LMS
6399

I.F. Carney

Noodle **N.B.** Books

© Ian Carney and Noodle Books 2012

ISBN 978-1-906419-70-7

First published in 2012 by Kevin Robertson
under the **NOODLE BOOKS** imprint
PO Box 279
Corhampton
SOUTHAMPTON
SO32 3ZX

www.noodlebooks.co.uk

Printed in England by Information Press Ltd. Oxford.

Above - *Fury, newly completed at the Hyde Park Works of the North British Locomotive Co. Ltd. A dozen workmen pretend to do things for the official photographer. (Getty Archive F9197A)*

(All unaccredited views have been sourced from unknown collections with no annotation as to ownership / copyright indicated.)

CONTENTS

PREFACE

A book on Fury was initially conceived because the locomotive was an intriguing example of engineering achievement and she had intrigued this author from his childhood. In the (very) many years since those childhood days, several writers have produced well-researched articles on segments of Fury's short life but the episodes had not before been collated and expanded into a single and reasonably complete narrative. Some compilers of previously published material have unknowingly perpetuated incorrect facts about Fury. So where possible I felt that correcting those errors was clearly worthwhile. Unfortunately some aspects of Fury's development and evaluation, especially the technical contributors to her construction, remain unknown (or uncertain) for now; but it has surprised me just how much hitherto buried material has been uncovered during the research.

Some 83 years have elapsed since Fury was first conceived and the people involved in her creation and testing are no longer around to consult. I was reliant therefore on archived material, both private and public. Hopefully, my research has not been superficial; it was conducted with enthusiasm and as much diligence as I could manage. If the inclusion of too many words like "possibly, probable or perhaps" within the text causes irritation then apologies are offered, but uncertainty was really unavoidable when so much of Fury's story remains obscure.

This is a book describing the short history of a special locomotive which existed for just a few years and was part of the search for steam "superpower". Fury was unique although she had a progenitor. Whilst some of the important socio-economic factors prevailing at the time had a bearing on Fury's genesis and ultimate fate, I have tried to limit these whilst still painting the broader picture of the society into which she was introduced with such high expectations.

The history of steam locomotives is a narrow discipline. Many of the books compiled in the 20th century have provided excellent technical accounts of some particular steam locomotive but seldom made more than passing reference to the economic or social influences which impinged on the engine's development and ultimate. The 21st century however has produced some first class studies combining the technology and impact of the railways on society. The excellent books by Ross [1] and the deservedly acclaimed *Fire & Steam* [2] by Wolmar are two such rich sources. They are examples of thorough research and a

readable style which I could not hope to emulate. For the reader who has not benefited from their wealth of knowledge, they are books to be recommended.

The advantage of studying an object through a microscope is that it shows detail not otherwise apparent. The disadvantage being that the object is viewed in a narrow perspective and isolated from its surroundings. Consequently, conclusions about the object of study may be drawn which are based on limited information. For historians, drawing conclusions from a narrow perspective can lead to presenting accurate information which is incomplete simply because the wider perspective has been insufficiently considered.

Additionally, the historian has a problem in maintaining objectivity. Information can be researched and collated but is difficult or even impossible sometimes to assess it without introducing a degree of personal prejudice, albeit unwittingly. Archived original letters or perhaps the official minutes of some meeting might be taken to represent a factual premise on which to build; yet they were no more than the original writer's interpretations of events with all the bias that is intrinsic in human nature.

The analyst of some significant piece of history may encourage the reader to reappraise the event but analysts of the same event will perceive it in different ways. No one account is definitive. Historians can seldom present truly objective analyses of events because they are dealing with human emotions and the profound but veiled way in which they influence history. At best they will present their readers with what they believe to be factual information in as

Opposite page - With the benefit of (computer) technology unavailable to the LMS and NBL, an indulgence into the realms of what might have been.

5

broader context as reasonably practical and lead them to challenge and interpret the evidence themselves.

Technology might be seen as a more focussed area than say economic or social history. But technology is never devoid of politics and economics. When Cossons compiled his book on industrial archaeology he sought to put the subject in the wider context of socio-political change and as a result the reader gains a better understanding of why the industrial revolution had to come about. He recognised that ". . . *there is a diffuse penumbra too, into which the industrial archaeologist must go to provide a perspective and context for his main area of interest.*" The industrial revolution did not just happen in isolation. It began because there was a socio-economic need and there were inventors clever and committed enough to pursue their ideas once demand was recognised.

The temptation for me to ignore the wider perspective of Fury's conception was appreciable, especially when inclusion of such material may be seen at best as peripheral or at worst, irrelevant by the reader. Yet to ignore it completely would be to look through the microscope and thus disregard that wider perspective.

One disadvantage of 'going down sidings' is that a strictly chronological approach is not really possible. The sequence must of necessity be broken as sometimes later events are examined so that their significance to the overall story may be appreciated.

I offer that too often repeated quotation of Sir Isaac Newton, *"If I have seen further it is only by standing on the shoulders of giants"* but with emphasis being placed on the "if".

I F Carney

Guildford 2011

ACKNOWLEDGMENTS

There is no doubt whatsoever that I could not have assembled this narrative and its images without the unqualified help afforded by a number of individuals. Therefore I owe them a great debt of gratitude.

Firstly to Kevin Robertson who as publisher encouraged throughout, helped no end and showed limitless patience.

Furthermore, Kevin provided one contact by which the necessary network of significant contributors was developed – Phil Atkins. It was he, who after retirement as librarian at the National Railway Museum (NRM) was of immense help to me. He facilitated the retrieval of important data at the NRM's "Search Engine". After that, Phil provided regular support and information from his encyclopaedic memory throughout the writing of this book. I cannot thank him enough.

I must also thank the staff at the NRM Search Engine, especially Grace Donaldson for her help during my visits.

In Glasgow, The Mitchell Library staff displayed patience with my constant enquiry and were very helpful given their difficulties of accessing old photographs and negatives. Unfortunately some images of Fury were lost in the transition of The Mitchell Library to "Glasgowlife". In the later stages of my research, Lynne Vezza was very accommodating in searching for obscure images from NBL for me.

The surviving original works drawings of Fury have been catalogued at The National Archives of Scotland. Their archivist, Alma Topen was of great assistance when I requested copies and for that, I repeat my thanks again to her.

I wish also to record thanks to Geoff Holt, that skilled producer of locomotive models (including Fury) and writer of one of the better articles on Fury. His friendliness and help was most welcome.

It was via Geoff that I was able to make contact with Nelson Twells, a fellow senior member of the LMS Society. Nelson was very generous with his time and provided me with many photographs of Fury in her later days from his personal collection. I am extremely grateful to him.

Alan Butcher of Ian Allan Publishing provided some key information and saved me considerable time. For that, I offer him my thanks.

Steam locomotive historians, whatever their "Big Four" allegiances, are a great fraternity to be involved with. I am glad to have had the opportunity to make contact with a few of them. I thank them for their enthusiasm and encouragement.

INTRODUCTION

The name "Fury" has been assigned throughout this story to its subject but having done so, some correcting explanation is necessary. The first locomotive to carry the name Fury predates our period of interest. Little is known of 2-2-0 Fury No. 1 beyond that she was a built in 1831 by Fenton & Murray for use on the Liverpool & Manchester Railway around 1839 and was a sister engine to Planet. Images of her appeared on lithographs and glazed pottery.

Fig. 0:1 The first locomotive to carry the Fury name shown on a pottery drinking mug from the 19th C.

Fig. 0:2 Fury of 1831.

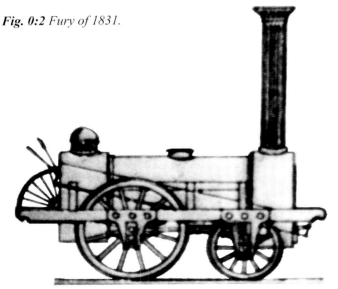

Many years later in the 1920s when the London Midland & Scottish Railway (LMS) began to assign names to their new 4-6-0 "Royal Scots" (henceforth simply the "Scots" as they became known), they chose to resurrect names of old locomotives such as *Planet, Ajax, Sans Pareil* and *Fury.* The Scot which was given the name Fury was numbered 6138. Other Scots were given the names of regiments in the British Army. This caused some indignant reactions from those regiments who felt slighted that their name did not appear on one of the LMS's new locomotives and they accordingly made their feelings known to the powers that be in the LMS. Thus it was that in December of 1929 *The Railway Magazine* carried a short announcement that *"In response to comments upon the omission of the name of the London Irish Rifle Regiment from the "Royal Scot" locomotives named after regiments, the L.M.S.R. has agreed to No. 6138, Fury, being renamed London Irish Rifleman."*

6138 Fury was not alone. Among others, the LMS found themselves transforming *Jenny Lind* to The Rifle Brigade; *Sans Pareil* became the Royal Army Service Corps; *Lion* was renamed The York & Lancaster Regiment, *Meteor* was changed to The Lovat Scouts (Fowler supported the Scout movement) and *Planet* lost her link to the past by becoming Royal Warwickshire Regiment. Those engines which did preserve the 'old names' when handed over to the LMS from the North British Locomotive Company (NBL) were given small handed brass plaques for fixing under the main curved name plate showing an outline of the old locomotive.

Fig. 0:3 Lieut.-Colonel Pilkington, in company with Sir Josiah Stamp, Mr J.H.Follows, Sir Henry Fowler, Mr C. Byrom and other officers of the L.M.S.R. on October 23rd 1929 as "re-christened" "Royal Scot" No. 6138, previously Fury, becomes The London Irish Rifleman".

By this time, October 1929, an experimental locomotive was already nearing completion at the North British Locomotive Company (NBL) and had been assigned the LMS number 6399. Since the LMS now found they had sets of redundant name plates in the stores, it would clearly save money to assign one to the new experimental 6399.

Whether "Fury" plates happened to be on top of the storeman's pile or whether the name was purposely selected we do not know. Whatever the explanation, our locomotive eventually emerged from NBL in early 1930 bearing the name Fury. Unfortunately, she was to be Fury by name and nature.

For convenience, the story to follow refers to that experimental locomotive as Fury before she was actually given the name.

Sir Henry Fowler was then the Chief Mechanical Engineer (CME) of the LMS and like most CMEs of railway companies, considered that he reigned unchallenged by the boards of directors in respect of locomotive design and development. It was Fowler who was described, inevitably but wrongly, as the designer of the Scots. But as CME, Fowler was undoubtedly instrumental in the creation of 6399 Fury and accordingly "Fowler's Fury" is an appropriate title for the story that follows.

Chapter One

HISTORICAL PERSPECTIVE

Commissioning a novel steam locomotive in the gloom of the British economy in the 1920s

The First World War had a dramatic effect on Britain and not just from the appalling loss of men throughout the 5 years of warfare. The total number of UK citizens killed in the period was 752,091. The enormous diversion of Britain's manufacturing output to armaments together with the post-war effects in other European countries had a profound effect on growth and investment in the UK.

In Britain the war's immediate consequences led to economic output falling by 25% between 1918 and 1921 and it did not recover until the end of the Great Depression around 1932.

It was hardly a good time to be investing in speculative engineering.

During the 1920s coalmining, steel and shipbuilding were the mainstay industries of Britain's export trade and these were located principally in the North of England, South Wales and central Scotland. These old but critical industries had to be sustained and new investment encouraged. What few new industries there were, such as motor cars, motor cycles and electrical goods were by contrast heavily concentrated in central and southern England. Their products needed to be moved from factories to consumers and to the docks for export and in the absence of effective road transport, the railways were key to business growth.

The industrial areas of Britain endured the 1920s in recession and the struggling industries actually received little investment or modernisation. Throughout the 1920s unemployment stayed at a steady one million when the total population in 1921 was 44 million.

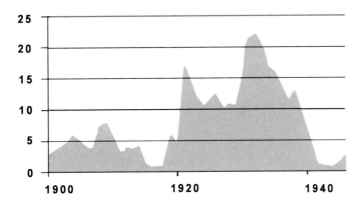

Fig. 1:1 UK Unemployment (%) between 1900 and 1940

Coupled with the stagnation and lack of investment, the dramatic rise in unemployment following the end of the war was a serious concern to the government of the day. At a cabinet meeting in August 1920 the minutes recorded [3]:-

"The Cabinet had before them a Joint Memorandum by the Minister of Health and the Minister of Labour (Paper C.P.1747)relating to Unemployment. It was stated that in the coming autumn the unemployment problem might constitute a serious danger, and that in order to try and lessen this danger it was necessary that the Government should be prepared with some scheme to provide employment during the winter months. There were ominous warnings that in certain trades, owing to lack of orders, there would be discharges on a large scale."

The 'serious danger' presumably referred to civil unrest as well as a drain on the country's diminishing monetary reserves. Coupled to this grim outlook for the unemployed worker in Britain, life expectancy during the 1920s was between 50 and 60 years (it is now 80).

Recognising that in the immediate post-war years the railways were vital means of moving goods, the government could not ignore the need for their development and of course, that their motive power was dependant on coal.

After government control during the war years, The Railway Act of 1921 restored the railways to private ownership and this created the regrouping of numerous small and medium sized railway companies into the 'big four' of LMS, LNER, GWR and Southern. This was at a time when Cabinet minutes from the early 1920s reveal the huge reductions in national expenditure that were being demanded for survival [4].

The British coal-mining industry suffered an economic crisis in 1925. Productivity was at its lowest ebb. Output per man had fallen to just 199 tons between 1920 and 1924. Before long, the mine owners announced their plans to cut miners' wages in an attempt to maintain their profits. In response, the TUC convened a special conference and announced that a general strike "in defence of miners' wages and hours" was to begin on 3 May 1926.

By October 1926 hardship forced many men back, especially those with young families. By the end of

November most miners were back at work and Britain's General Strike was over.

Perhaps surprisingly, in all the 100 years from 1900 to 2000, days lost to strikes peaked in 1926 at 160 million.

"The Great Depression"

This term was coined to describe the severe worldwide economic depression which lasted throughout the 1930s. It was to be the longest and deepest economic downturn of the 20th century.

Similar to the recession of the early 21st century, the Great Depression began in the United States. On "Black Tuesday", October 29, 1929 the US stock market collapsed and within

a short time, the consequences reverberated around the world. These were manifest as big rises in unemployment leading to falls in personal income, fiscal reduction and a catastrophic decline in world trade.

Just 18 days before Black Tuesday, Sir Henry Fowler had asked the LMS for approval to build Fury.

The northern industrial areas of Britain were immediately affected because demand for their traditional industrial products collapsed. By the end of 1930 unemployment had risen from 1 million to 2.5 million or 20% of the workforce. In some towns and cities of the north east of England, as ship yards faced a 90% reduction in orders, unemployment reached 70%. Within 3 years of the start of the depression, 30% of Glaswegians previously employed in heavy industry

Fig. 1:2 Four railway company posters from the 1920s depicting attempts to lure the rich and poor alike onto trains. Despite the gloom, the population was being encouraged to travel or as the Southern Railway would have it – escape to Winter Sunshine. Though just where this sunshine might be and who could afford to seek it was another matter. The LMS meanwhile introduced a new set of posters in 1928 promoting their parcels services.

were unemployed. Fury was to be built in Glasgow.

By contrast, the Midlands and South of England had less dependency on heavy industry and the effects of the depression were not so severe. In fact by the mid-1930s there was increasing prosperity. However Britain was fast becoming aware that other countries were introducing new ideas in transport irrespective of the continuing austerity.

Germany had launched the two new transatlantic liners *Bremen* and *Europa* into service. *Bremen* was launched 2 August 1928 and with her sister ship, were considered at that time as the most modern liners in the world. Their characteristics were high speeds and luxury. Naturally Britain did not want to be left out in the shipbuilding race so Cunard planned a 75,000 ton ship of their own. Construction of the liner began in December 1930 at John Brown & Company Shipbuilding and Engineering shipyard at Clydebank in Scotland. As shown in Fig 4, this was at the

peak of unemployment. In December 1931 as a result of the Great Depression the government supplied a loan to complete the ship. Thus *Queen Mary* and later, *Queen Elizabeth* were launched.

In this part of Scotland another giant of manufacturing was suffering greatly during the depression. The North British Locomotive Company, which was pivotal in the story of Fury, had seen its profits drop some 97% from 1925 to 1929. Worse was to follow for the company and it was not until the outbreak of WWII in 1939 that the company again began to declare profits from its operations[1].

The relevance of this background to the story of Fury will become apparent when the conflicting pressures on the LMS to conserve money and grow the business are considered. As a result of "the grouping" the new LMS acquired the biggest problems.

Year	shillings	pence
1920	61	5
1921	39	5
1922	26	2
1923	28	0
1924	27	3
1925	25	1
1926	21	11
1927	21	4
1928	18	8
1929	19	0
1930	19	7

Fig. 1:3 Large Steam Coal: Price per ton f.o.b. at Cardiff [6]

But the none of the railway companies was isolated from the prevailing economic situation in the mid 1920s and one result was that no expansion of track was taking place.

Between 1900 to 1925 total UK track length had increased by just 150 miles [5].

It is frequently claimed that at this time, the price of coal continued to rise and this, along with other material costs, was hitting the railway companies hard. Furthermore it is often stated that the price of coal was now a significant factor in the operating costs of the railway companies and if the consumption of coal per mile could be reduced then their competitivenes could be improved. Yet the table opposite shows that the price of Welsh steam coal fell steadily throughout the decade. In 1928, this particular fuel of choice for locomotives was being sold at less than half the price it had been just 7 years earlier.

But such raw data can be misleading because the railway companies could afford neither the time nor costs of bringing their coal from Cardiff. Instead they were dependant on coal which was mined close to their operating depots. In many cases the locally produced coal was of a poor quality for burning in locomotives and steaming suffered as a consequence. Additionally a locomotive could receive coal of variable quality over a long journey through different coalfields and improving efficiency of the locomotive was still of prime importance to the railway companies.

Nevertheless, other than the two short dips in production with the miners' and General Strike, coal production was as high as ever [5]. Steam locomotives faced no shortages of fuel whatever the variability of its quality for steam raising.

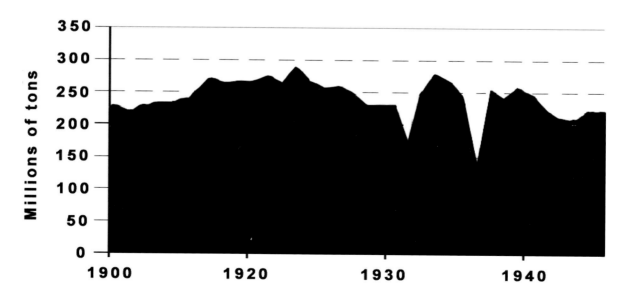

Coal Production in the UK: 1900-1940

Fig. 1:4 (opposite page lower left & (right) Showing how in the early 1920s coal production remained high whilst there was a dramatic fall in retail prices expressed as year-on-year change.

Change in Prices on Previous Year

Overall, the year-on-year price changes reveal that 1920 was a crisis year for the British economy. As part of the drastic war measures the railway companies had lost millions of pounds after the Great War. The government legislated on prices in July 1920 and doubled railway fares and freight charges. The unexpected consequence was that this reduced the income of the railways still further because austerity was reducing passenger numbers and goods traffic anyway.

Against this background, the late 1920s found the railway companies still coming to terms with the appreciable problems of being forced together into the new 'big four' grouping (except the GWR which had little problem assimilating smaller rivals). Their profits were falling,

passenger numbers were falling and yet they seemed expansionist in outlook. The contemporary railway journals carried hundreds of articles describing new stations, goods yards, export of locomotives and significantly, new locomotives. They were also devoting pages, no doubt prompted by the railway companies, to new efforts in experimentation to see if increases in efficiency (i.e. more power for less cost) could be realised.

Railways in the UK were confronting much the same issues as those in other countries of Europe. Amidst the prevailing economic gloom of the 1920s a number of far-sighted engineers were looking to develop new designs of steam locomotives.

Fig. 2:1 First Scot off the production line at NBL posing in shop grey for the official works photograph. The diamond shaped plate on the smoke box shows this to be the real 6100 and not 6125 masquerading as 6100, the first Scot. The LMS had earlier tried that deception.

Fig. 2:2 Layout of works at Glasgow

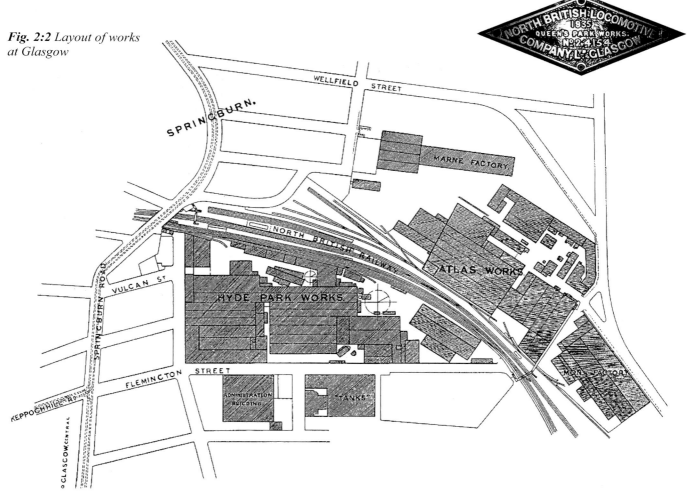

NBL - HYDE PARK (AND ATLAS) WORKS

Chapter Two

LMS, THE SCOTS AND SOMETHING NEW

The search for "superpower" higher pressures and Compound working

Following the Railways Act of 1921, the grouping of the numerous and varied railway undertakings into the Big Four companies had been by and large accomplished in 1923. For the largest of the Big Four, the new LMS Railway, its problems were legion.

It had acquired 34 separate companies, about 7,000 miles of track and found it employed the largest number of employees at a staggering 275,000 (by March of 1929, it was still the biggest employer of the Big Four but with 30,000 fewer).

The LMS was a business shambles after grouping. The 34 component companies still retained their own ways of working and in many cases, these were years out of date – as were their locomotives. But three years later, principally due to the appointment of the autocratic Sir Josiah Stamp as chairman, improvements in integration began. Stamp immediately set about remedying their aged engines and particularly the evident deficiency in all types of big locomotives. It didn't demand much perspicacity to recognise that whereas other companies could run their new fast expresses with existing locomotives, the LMS was still dependent on the inefficient 'double heading' whereby two less powerful engines had to be coupled together over much of the newly acquired LMS rail network. Enforced double heading on the scale practiced in the LMS was a huge disadvantage compared to rival companies. It increased running costs through using extra skilled manpower and increased overall coal consumption on any route and slowed journey times. Understandably, double heading created an impression with the passengers of an antiquated service compared with other companies such as the LNER operating over competing routes.

Fowler had been appointed in 1925 but history judges that he was not really successful at integrating the LMS component companies into a unified organisation for design and construction [45].

Although the economic climate was not conducive to major investment in new engines, unless a quick solution was to be found to this deficiency the LMS would lose even more revenue and status to the other companies.

Some historians record that Stamp turned to his CME Henry Fowler and directed him to design a new class of fast,

Fig. 2:3 Sir Henry Fowler, KBE, LLD, (1870- 1938) President of the Institution of Mechanical Engineers, Chief Mechanical Engineer of the London Midland and Scottish Railway.

powerful locomotives which were capable of providing the new long distance, express passenger services.

Sixsmith [7] describes the internal stresses within the LMS after grouping and is dismissive of any key role for the CME in the design of the new locomotives which were to become "The Scots". For those seeking a comprehensive account of the Scots' origins and development, Sixsmith's book may be consulted.

But it was not until December 1925 that Fowler formally asked that the LMS board agree to his proposal to construct

50 "improved 4-6-0 passenger tender engines" at an estimated total cost of £387,500". This would be equivalent to about £12,000,000 in 2011[11]. The LMS agreed to go forward in line with Fowler's proposal.

It is interesting to note that at this stage, a 4-6-0 was specifically mentioned in the proposal. The first 4-6-0 in Britain appeared in 1894 and although other wheel configurations were popular, it was Churchward of the GWR who demonstrated the effectiveness of the 4-6-0 despite the constraints it imposed on firebox size. By 1925 NBL had built hundreds of this type, mainly for export.

The 4-6-0 configuration had much to commend it to the LMS. Such locomotives were shorter than a 4-6-2 (Pacific) and existing turntables and maintenance arrangements would not require modification. It was also believed, with justification, that the 4-6-0 was less prone to wheel slip since as a train begin to move, the locomotive's weight was transferred backwards and without a rear bogie, this downward force was exerted on the rear, coupled driving wheels.

After delay and dithering the LMS management then used the old ploy of seeking more information to avoid drawing up a firm order from Fowler's proposal. They agreed to examine first just what the competition could achieve in terms of locomotive performance. They sought and perhaps surprisingly obtained the loan of one of the GWR's new Castle class engines. This move again reflects the dilatory nature of LMS decision making since earlier in 1925 Gresley of the LNER had been able to compare a Castle with the performance of his own 4-6-2 Pacific.

The Castles were a logical development of earlier GWR 'Star' designs by their CME Charles Collett. A new No. 8 boiler working at 225 psi was introduced by Swindon and the total design was a great success from the start, producing a tractive effort of 31,625 lbs (14,182 kg) from 4 cylinders. At their introduction the Castles were the most powerful engines in Britain. The first locomotive was Caerphilly Castle built in August of 1923.

Two years later the LMS were still vacillating about what to do.

The 4-6-0 GWR Launceston Castle was made available to the LMS for trials in October 1926, a full ten months after the board's acceptance of Fowler's proposal. The overwhelming superiority of the GWR locomotive's performance on LMS metals led the board, undoubtedly with Fowler's agreement, to endorse their earlier commitment for a new 4-6-0 engine of their own. This outcome could surely have been foreseen at least two years earlier.

Controversy still exists about what happened next. There are claims that after an unsuccessful attempt to persuade the Great Western Railway to provide drawings for the Castles, drawings of the Southern Railway's 4-6-0 were provided and these were passed to the drawing office (D.O.) of the LMS Derby Works from which a design for a "new" 4-6-0 locomotive was to emerge.

However, John Court, Projects Manager at the North British Locomotive works (to whom we will return later) disputes this [10] stating that the Derby D.O. paid no attention to the Southern's drawings and developed the Scot drawings de novo.

In his history of NBL[8], Bradley however records a different story from Court. His research showed that the design was worked out by NBL "by borrowing a full set of drawings from the Southern Railway". These S.R. drawings would have been for their King Arthur class which NBL had already built. Perhaps that was why NBL could execute the order for the Scots in such a short time.

The official order for 235 new LMS locomotives comprising 5 new classes, including the 50 Scots, was dated 10th December 1926 – a whole year after the original agreement was given to proceed. Bradley states that the NBL Drawing Office Register shows the date of the order as Christmas Day 1926[8]. Reed wrote that the actual order to an agreed price for the Scots was not signed until February 27th 1927 [9]. So after all the delay, of which Fowler must share the blame, the LMS then demanded the seemingly impossible - that NBL provide the locomotives to be in service during late 1927.

Reed [9] also wrote that Fowler had been "over-ridden" with respect to the basic Scot design. Apparently although orders were issued above his signature, he played little part in either the design or contract, confirming Bradley's account (above). Shortly after his appointment to CME in 1925, Fowler was contemplating a compound 4-6-2 and subsequently much of the design element of his CME job was passed to Anderson at Derby [9]. We may reasonably conclude that Fowler's role in the design of the Scots was minimal, especially given Bradley's research that the designs were developed at NBL.

Their construction would not have been possible within any of the LMS workshops which were heavily committed to other builds and the repair of inherited, old and worn engines. The order was therefore given to the North British Locomotive Company Ltd in Glasgow. NBL, which despite their enormous experience in building locomotives since 1903, were faced with a severe decline in their profitability. In 1925 their declared profits were a mere £113,807 yet when the final, priced LMS order was received in 1927, their profit had dropped to just £7,622. In the following year whilst the Scots were being constructed, profits were a paltry £317. NBL was close to extinction and declared profits were actually produced by transferring huge sums from reserves [8]. Between 1905 and 1932 the North British Locomotive Company's production of engines had dropped from 573 per year to only 16.

There were many factors contributing to this situation which were beyond the control of contract builders such as NBL. The component costs of a steam locomotive were represented by materials (50 to 70%), wages (20 to 30%) and, if built in-house, 'works charges' or profit if built by contractors. Works charges were often based on creative accounting and as a result building new engines in the railway companies' own workshops appeared less costly. For example, in 1925 the cost of building an LMS 4-4-0 in their own works was between £5,604 and £6,456 whereas contractors were asking £6,547 to £6,651 per locomotive [45]. This was at a time when materials cost had been fairly static for many years.

The LMS order for the 50 Scots would therefore have been very welcome to the directors of NBL and possibly represented their salvation thanks to the inability of LMS workshops to do the job. NBL fulfilled their part of the contract admirably. They divided the order equally between their two principle works in Glasgow – Hyde Park and Queen's Park. The locomotives from each works bearing characteristic circular maker's plates and diamond shaped maker's plates respectively.

After completion, all engines would have been delivered via Queen's Park Works direct to Polmadie shed for running in and onward transit south. One source claims it is possible that final erection of the whole batch of 50 took place at Queen's Park, but this cannot be confirmed.

Incredibly the first Scot (No. 6100 "Royal Scot") was available for the LMS on July 14th 1927 – less than 5 months after the final cost agreement had been signed.

Attention to the Scots is important because it was from the basic design of these new locomotives that Fury was to eventually emerge 3 years later.

Fig. 2:4 6105 'Cameron Highlander' at Camden.

Chapter Three

EXPERIMENTS WITH HIGH PRESSURE FOR "SUPERPOWER"

Producing more motive energy from coal in ultra high pressure steam locomotives

Carnot in 1834 had set down the principles of engine efficiency and years after his death, the application of his thesis to steam engines was realised. If more heat could be created *i.e. with hotter steam* then improvement in engine efficiency would result.

In theory a 100% efficient engine would convert all the energy put into it as rotational motion at the wheels; no heat would be lost as wasted energy. This cannot be realised in practice of course as energy is used up in overcoming the internal friction of moving parts and heating up the system to its equilibrated, working temperature. In a typical steam engine, heat was derived from the burning fuel (usually coal in Europe) and large amounts of its latent energy was used to first heat up the whole boiler structure and its water content. After which it had to then to raise the temperature of the water sufficiently to generate steam which could be used to create 'locomotion' via the locomotive's moving parts.

As early as 1781[1] it was shown possible to extract more useful work from the steam which was otherwise escaping from the cylinder after moving the piston. In the process known as compound working, this exhausted steam from one cylinder is piped into other cylinders of larger size where more work could be done although at lower pressure. There was precedent enough for this from steam generation in marine engines. The first steamships so equipped dated from around 1870 in which compound working was employed.

This was in contrast to simple working where exhaust steam was not re-used, as in most locomotives of that date.

Compounding was an attractive proposition for locomotives; it "only" required larger cylinders for the second stage as well as higher initial boiler pressure. The benefits were perceived to include smoother running and more work from less coal.

There were major challenges though. In practice, the application could not easily be adapted for use in a steam locomotive. Generating steam at significantly higher temperature and pressure would have required traditional locomotive boilers to be impractically strong and heavy with the materials and construction of the day.

Marine boilers were fundamentally different from locomotive boilers and not just in terms of size and weight. The former had water-tube boilers the latter had fire-tube boilers. Marine, water-tube boilers could be built for rigid ships where weight was not an issue, whereas fitting them into a locomotive with its inherent flexing and where weight was an important consideration, required new thinking. In addition, locomotive boilers in contrast to marine boilers, are always undergoing significant changes in internal pressure as the engine is worked and this causes further flexing and structural stresses. Expansion of any boiler (particularly lengthwise) as it is started up is appreciable and for use in stationary and marine engines, this can be accommodated with relative ease. By contrast, steam locomotives with their constantly varying pressure and temperature over a journey the expansion problems are more difficult to overcome; especially when the inevitable buffeting occurs as the train is constantly accelerated and stopped. Not surprisingly locomotive water-tube boilers were prone to develop leaks which were difficult and expensive to repair.

Opposite page, experiments with high-pressure steam in Germany.

Top - *Fig. 3:1 H17-206 of 1925, coal fired compound with a boiler pressure of 1,000psi. The long steam, drum is above the firebox.*

Bottom - *Fig. 3:2 HO2-1001 of 1929. Very small hp cylinders provided with steam at 1,750 psi, ahead of the driving wheels: the chimney is also set back above the leading driving wheels. Single low pressure inside cylinder. A coal saving of 42% was guaranteed by the manufacturers. In practice any increase in efficiency was small compared with the greatly increased costs.*

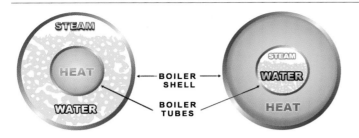

Fig. 3:3 Simple diagram to illustrate the difference between a fire-tube boiler (left) and a water-tube boiler (right).

Improving efficiency now presented a problem for locomotive engineers. Generating steam at high pressure for compound working required adaption of the marine water-tube boiler to the constraints of locomotive frames and loading gauges. The loading gauge constraint was tighter in Britain than elsewhere in the world where new engines were being built. The USA probably had the most generous allowances. Compounding had been tried many times before in locomotives, notably by Webb in 1882 of the L&NW Railway (to become part of the LMS). In all cases though 'normal' steam pressures, produced from a regular fire-tube boiler had been used. Efficiency was improved but often at the cost of higher maintenance and reduced reliability.

There was no precise definition of what a "high pressure" steam boiler represented. From about 1850 onwards, boilers had been pressed to higher duty and by around 1900 engines were operating around 150 psi (1Pa or $1N/m^2$). By the time the Scots were built using 250 psi boilers, a high pressure boiler would have been considered to operate at over 350 psi.

Yet despite these improvements, the steam locomotive of the early 1920s was a very inefficient machine. At best, it might have had an overall efficiency of around 5% meaning that theoretically 95% of the potential energy input was being wasted.

Given this starting position, to effect even a modest improvement in efficiency would produce worthwhile savings in running costs.

The Water-Tube Boiler in a Steam Locomotive.

Although the marine type of water tube boiler was stronger, there were those significant difficulties in adapting it for use in a locomotive. In addition to the aforementioned flexing of locomotive frames, the biggest concern was that of corrosion and the associated problem of scale. Both of these factors can lead to catastrophic failure of a boiler under pressure and in the mid 1920s no reliable methods were available to monitor the progressive effects of scale build up and corrosion.

Scale builds up in a boiler over time due to the deposition of salts from impure water. In essence that means hard water in which soluble salts are converted to insoluble ones. The scale inhibits heat transfer and causes localised heat build up which distorts and weakens the structure of the boiler.

In 1910 it was already clear that to overcome corrosion and scale, the use of pure water in the boiler was essential.

By 1920 it had become clear that boiler corrosion was caused by a combination of factors and not just variations in pH (acidity / alkalinity) of the water used. For by now the effects of dissolved oxygen and carbon dioxide had been identified as causative agents and these were much more difficult to manage. Although failure of a water tube boiler on a ship was a significant enough event, such an occurrence in a railway locomotive could be catastrophic for bystanders and especially the footplate crew who had control of a train with perhaps several hundred passengers on board.

The Schmidt System

One solution to the scale problem was developed by Dr Wilhelm Schmidt. He was born in Germany in 1858 and when 36, he published details of a compound engine using high temperature steam.

Schmidt is claimed to have made "the last great contribution to the development of the steam locomotive"[1]. Though this must be a controversial claim, he certainly brought about very significant improvements in performance and efficiency.

The Schmidt system used a closed ultra-high pressure system containing steam which then gave up its heat to raise the temperature of water in a second vessel. This second vessel was in effect a high pressure boiler from which steam was extracted to drive the pistons. With this arrangement, the Schmidt system solved the problem of scale and corrosion by indirect heating of pure water in a closed loop and it extracted more energy from the steam because it was generated at much higher pressure.

(In German, Heissdampf *(Heißdampf)* means 'hot steam' and amusingly Ross informed his readers[1] that Wilhelm Schmidt was known to his work colleagues as Heissdampf Willi or "Hot Steam Willy").

It is important at this stage to appreciate how this complex arrangement worked in practice. Without adequate explanation and understanding, the later events of Fury's story may not be fully appreciated.

Although subsequent pictures of Fury's boiler appear to show very complex structures, the principle of the operation

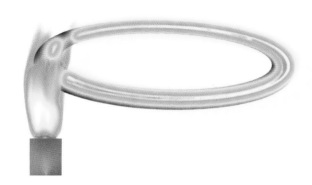

Fig. 3:4

is quite simple and the diagrams should explain the basics.

The basis of the Schmidt system was to put a quantity of purified water inside a sealed loop capable of withstanding the "ultra" high pressure which would be produced *(Fig.3:4)*.

Continuous application of heat would clearly raise the internal pressure to very high levels as no escape of the enclosed steam was permitted. If the heat could not escape from the hollow ring either then it would quickly become "red hot".

However, if the loop containing its ultra high pressure steam is passed through a second vessel containing water, this will boil to produce steam *(Fig.3:5)*.

Now that heat is being extracted from the hollow ring, eventually equilibrium will be reached where virtually all the supplied heat will be used to boil the water. In the Schmidt system, the steam produced from the second boiler was used to do two things. About 25% of this steam was withdrawn for powering the high pressure cylinder and producing motion. The bulk was recycled through the steam generator to produce more steam. This steam condensed to produce water of high purity.

Originally, exhaust steam from the high pressure cylinder was led to a lower pressure boiler which was not heated by the fire or its hot gases but by this exhausted high pressure steam which had already done some work. This lower pressure boiler in fact produced steam at 225 psi and from there, after more superheating, dry steam was passed to the low pressure cylinders of the locomotive. Later designs allowed for the low pressure boiler (a traditional fire tube boiler) to be heated via the hot gases from the firebox.

Taking the simplification to the next stage, in a locomotive the closed loop was actually the foundation ring and tubes which surrounded the burning fuel, usually coal. The remote boiler through which the closed loop passed was a large and immensely strong high pressure drum mounted above the firebox.

Those high pressure tubes which lined the firebox contained steam 'superheated' to about 900°F (488°C) which caused the internal pressure to rise to 1700 psi (117 bar) or equivalent to a force of 120kg per square cm or a bit less than 1 ton per sq inch acting on all the tubes!

Additionally, in this immensely complicated Schmidt system, the pure water needed for the high pressure steam generator was produced from the exhausted steam leaving the high pressure cylinder being condensed in the low pressure boiler. It was not therefore truly closed at all but one into which fresh purified water was pumped.

Schmidt had his own company, the *Schmidt'sche Heißdampf Gesselschaft* and at some point in the mid 1920s he decided to collaborate with Henschels to convert a 4-6-0 Prussian locomotive such that the inner, third cylinder would operate at the very high steam pressure but the two outer cylinders used steam at lower, more normal pressure.

It first appeared as the 'Schwarzkopff-Löffler' a name reflecting both the builders and designer respectively. Its declared purpose was to improve fuel economy, with the added benefit of increasing the locomotive's power within the constraints of the German loading gauge. It was shown at the Transport Exhibition in 1925 although it was not properly tested until late 1926 at the Grunewald facility [10]. A later version was the HO2-1001 *(Fig.3:2)*.

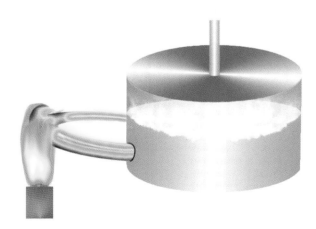

Fig. 3:5

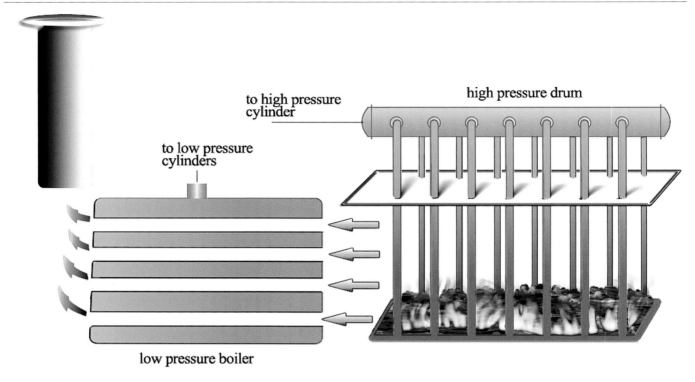

to high pressure cylinder

high pressure drum

to low pressure cylinders

low pressure boiler

Fig. 3:6 Diagrammatic representation of the Schmidt system in a locomotive.

As noted earlier, in that year, this first "International German Transport Exhibition" in Munich showed the state-of-the-art of technology of the day. Exhibitors from Germany and Austria in particular presented their latest developments in all forms of transport[13]. H17-206 was amongst the exhibits.

At the exhibition the locomotive and its boiler reportedly aroused the interest of attendees from The Superheater Company [10].

This American company had developed rapidly from its origins in the 19th century but there is contradictory

Fig. 3:7 Opposite side of H17-206 built by Henschel in 1925 operating at a steam pressure of 1000 psi.

information about its involvement with Schmidt.

According to Ross, in 1910 Schmidt had sold them the patent for his superheater[1]. But this does not tally with other reports that the Combustion Engineering Company formed a partnership with the Superheater Company to form 'The Locomotive Superheater Company' in 1910 "to further the use of superheated steam in locomotives".

A more authoritative account, since it was written by the technical staff of the Superheater Company in 1932, states that In 1902, when Schmidt announced his superheater, this led to the formation of the joint Schmidt Superheating Company Ltd in 1908 "for the purpose of developing the use of this design in Great Britain".

Two years later in 1910, Schmidt's success in Europe resulted in the formation of The Locomotive Superheater Company (later known just as The Superheater Company) in the United States, in order to develop the use of his apparatus in that country.

The Schmidt Superheating Co Ltd., was reorganised in 1919, and renamed the Marine and Locomotive Superheaters Ltd. and finally, in 1924, after amalgamation with the Superheater Corporation, Ltd., assumed its present title of The Superheater Company Ltd.[14]

By then it had already developed a close relationship with the LMS supplying it with numerous locomotive superheaters *(Fig.3:9)*.

So in early 1928, whilst the LMS was basking in the glory of the new Scots' performance, Fowler was having to think hard about events taking place elsewhere. The stimulus had been the 1925 Munich Railway Exhibition and Fowler's interest had clearly been aroused.

The Superheater Company Ltd was to play a key role in the genesis of Fury and the LMS's drive for 'superpower'. Without their initiative it is certain that the LMS would not have contemplated embarking on the development of such an experimental locomotive.

Top - Fig 3:8 Munich Transport Exhibition Brochure. Reproduced by kind permission of David Levine [13]

Right - Fig 3:9 Promoting links between the LMS and Superheater Company Ltd, notwithstanding the spurious percentages!

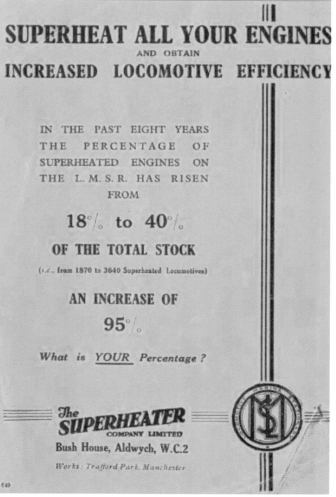

Chapter Four

FURY - ORIGINS and COMMISSIONING

NBL, and Superheater Company, the contractual issues

The Superheater Company Ltd had obtained the licence from Schmidt'sche Heissdampf Gesellschaft and as recounted by Court (remember he was Head of Projects at NBL), *"The construction of a locomotive similar to the German prototype was agreed upon, 'for completion in 1929' by the Superheater Co. and the L.M.S."*

Why in 1928 did Fowler commit the LMS to an experiment when the economy in Britain was in such a poor state, unemployment was high and passenger income low, yet coal production remained high and its price comparatively low?

Why did the board of the LMS acquiesce to Fowler's proposal when the company's finances were in as poor a state as the national economy?

Fowler had just earlier got them to agree to spend millions of pounds on new locomotives. As seen in Chapter 1, the government had fixed fares, railway revenue had declined and the outlook for railways was grim. It was just 5 years after the enforced 'grouping' and the LMS was struggling to assimilate disparate and troublesome companies within its structure. It hardly seemed the time for the CME to be embarking on speculative research.

For Fowler however there were probably a number of reasons why he was prepared to persuade the LMS board to endorse this project to build an experimental locomotive.

In 1921, just 7 years before, he had been extolling the virtues of superheating at the prestigious Institution of Mechanical Engineers [16]. He would have been aware also that SNCF (the French National Railway) had responded to the Henschel H17-206 locomotive at the Munich exhibition by securing agreement to adapt a 4-8-2 PLM locomotive to incorporate the new boiler. The eventual fate of which will be of relevance in the unfolding story of Fury.

In addition, Leonore F Loree, president of the Delaware & Hudson Railway in the USA had begun in 1923 to build a 4-8-0 locomotive which had a high pressure boiler using water tube construction. From the beginning, Loree claimed that his engine would "burn 30% less coal to do an equivalent amount of work as a conventional engine". (However in practice its complexity meant maintenance cost negated any

saving in coal consumption).

The Delaware & Hudson Railway continued development with three further locomotives, with increasingly higher boiler pressures and little attempt seems to have been made to keep these developments confidential.

Fowler's opposite number, Nigel Gresley - CME of the rival LNER had taken a particular interest in the performance of the American engines and in 1924 he and Yarrow Shipbuilders Ltd entered a 3 year partnership to develop a British high pressure locomotive using the obligatory water-tube boiler. Despite the secrecy surrounding this project (the locomotive was known as the 'hush-hush'), it is inconceivable that Fowler had not got wind of it.

But no secrecy surrounded Gresley's address in 1925 to the Institute of Mechanical Engineers on 3 cylinder, high pressure locomotives wherein he listed their evident advantages [17]. Fowler made his own input after Gresley's address "commenting on other high pressure locomotives".

Whether Fowler was also aware of any Great Western Railway interest in high pressure locomotives is less clear. The NRM archives contain a copy of an 8 page report by Dr Herbert Brown M.I.L.E. of comparative trials between the Swiss Winterthur high pressure locomotive and another standard locomotive. Intriguingly, this copy bears the stamp of the GWR CME's Department and is dated December 1928. The report showed details of the Winterthur engine operating at 850 psi and commented that the Winterthur locomotive showed coal savings "as high as 30.5%" and it "gave full satisfaction". Comparisons were also drawn with the data obtained from the Schmidt locomotive.
We can assume that Swindon was not convinced.

Herbert Brown had also published in 1928, this time in the prestigious Journal of the Institution of Locomotive Engineers. His paper was No. 237 "High pressure locomotives 655-86. Disc.: 686-92. Swiss Locomotive Company".

There could be no doubt that the high pressure locomotive was in vogue.

Opposite page - *Fig. 4:1 An imposing 'head on' view of Fury taken as part of the short sequence of official photographs taken at Hyde Park Works. (Getty Archive G961)*

Fig. 4:2 *Gresley's 4-6-4 No. 10000.*

In 1927, Fowler was elected President of the Institute of Mechanical Engineers. We can be certain therefore that Fowler, as any CME should be, was well informed about new locomotive technology in 1928 and the interest of other companies in such developments. Irrespective of any pique he may have felt over the LMS's failure to pursue his plans for a Pacific compound some years earlier, he would have wanted his company to be part of the super high pressure action. He would have been conscious of the LMS being left behind if it had not an equivalent investigation underway.

Ignoring the German, French, Swiss, American, LNER and later Canadian activities with super high pressure boilers was therefore not really an option for Fowler and the LMS. Accordingly, when the Superheater Company approached him with an offer to build a special boiler based on their Schmidt patent; Fowler would have been very receptive despite the economic situation within his company and country.

On October 11th of 1928 Fowler therefore wrote to the LMS Locomotive & Electrical Committee, referring to the Schmidt system [7]:-

"There is no doubt that there is a general tendency through the locomotive world to move in the direction of much higher steam pressures, and I am of the opinion that if the proposals are looked upon in the lines of research, it would be advantageous for us to make a trial of the same type of locomotive"

Sixsmith [7] recounts that Fowler backed this up with a claim that a 20% reduction in coal consumption would result, saving between £130 and £140 per annum per engine.

Perhaps Fowler concocted these figures from Loree's claims in the USA but they are hardly convincing as he offered no data either on the cost of building such engines or their maintenance, which Fowler would have, or certainly should have, known to be much higher than normal.

In fact the LMS wrung a very favourable contract from the Superheater Company which would anyway have been prepared to support development costs of a complete locomotive with the expectation of further orders coming their way for boilers. Fowler estimated the cost of the 'one off' boiler to be £3,000 but he had agreed with the Superheater Company that the LMS contribution would be limited to half that - but significantly - only if the locomotive was found to be satisfactory in service. The LMS therefore had got themselves an attractive, advantageous and low-cost project

Subsequent research by Dunbar at the Scottish Record Office, reported in 1976 [16] revealed details of this agreement. It is worthy of study. This author's comments are in parentheses:-

The first clause stated that "the L.M.S. Company should place free of charge at the Superheater Company's disposal a complete undercarriage comprising frame, wheels, axles, cylinders, cab splashers and panels together with a suitable tender this to known hereafter as the Chassis". *(This was to be one of the Scots and would be built at NBL).*

The Superheater Company undertook to "design and fit to the chassis within a reasonable period of time a high pressure two pressure boiler hereafter termed a boiler based on the patents of the Schmidtische *(sic)* Heissdampf GmbH and will assume full responsibility insofar as the patent position is concerned". *(Little financial risk attached to the LMS here; they would always have a Scot chassis if The Superheater Company failed to deliver a working boiler).*

"The boiler was to be made by the NBL Company and all assistance in supervision and testing of materials was to be given free of charge by the LMS. The CME of that concern would have submitted for approval all designs and specifications, analyses and tests which the Superheater Company intended to be used in the boiler construction. All subcontractors' names had to be likewise submitted for approval. When the boiler was fitted the usual tests had to take place at the works of the NBL. These consisting of the usual hydraulic and steam tests with the locomotive to be run on rollers."

"On these tests being concluded to the satisfaction of the CME the railway shall within 14 days take over the entire charge of the locomotive subject to the following conditions:- The Railway company shall then at its own expense carry out such tests and trials as it, jointly with the Superheater Company, consider desirable to arrive at the efficiency of the boiler and locomotive". Such tests were to be completed within six months from the date of taking over the engine, while reasonable allowance would be made for unforeseen circumstances arising. *(The overall responsibility for the boiler clearly was to reside with Fowler – he had to approve the design and importantly, the materials used).*

"Arising from the trials any alterations or improvements which may be jointly agreed to be desirable to carry out on the boiler during the trials would be at the expense of the Superheater Company, while those on the chassis shall be borne by the Railway company".
(Again, the LMS were getting off very lightly – they were only responsible for paying for rectification of the proven Scot running chassis).

"After the engine had been placed in traffic and found to be performing quite satisfactorily it would then be taken over entirely by the Railway Company". *(This clause was to prove a thorn in the side of the LMS. The definitions of "placed in traffic" and "quite satisfactorily" were just too vague).*

Clause 5 of the agreement retained at the NRM seems at variance with the above. This stated that once the boiler testing was completed to Fowler's satisfaction, the LMS would assume full responsibility for the engine within 2 weeks. This provoked one LMS reviewer of the agreement to express his objection:-

"The locomotive when fitted with the boiler shall undergo the usual tests at the North British Locomotive Co's Works, that is, the boiler shall be tested hydraulically and with steam, and the locomotive shall be run on rollers. When these tests have been approved by the Chief Mechanical Engineer of the Railway, the Railway shall, within 14 days, take over entire charge of the locomotive subject to the following:-" *(- extract from NRM records.)*

The Superheater Company must have been particularly committed to the Schmidt boiler and since the LMS were the most likely big customer in the UK, the Superheater

Fig. 4:3 *The Delaware and Hudson 4-8-0 being inspected but seemingly also derailed.*

Company were prepared to sign up to a joint venture where the financial risks were almost entirely theirs.

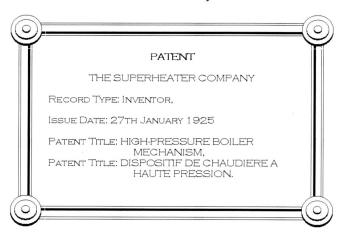

PATENT

THE SUPERHEATER COMPANY

RECORD TYPE: INVENTOR,

ISSUE DATE: 27TH JANUARY 1925

PATENT TITLE: HIGH-PRESSURE BOILER
MECHANISM,
PATENT TITLE: DISPOSITIF DE CHAUDIERE A
HAUTE PRESSION.

It would have been appropriate that the CME would have had final responsibility for a locomotive that would run on his company's metals and Fowler's requirement to approve all aspects of the Superheater Company's boiler was understandable.

What is uncertain however is the extent to which Fowler discharged his responsibilities in this regard. A man in his position would have been expected to delegate and indeed he passed the day-to-day supervision of the boiler's construction to Frank Pepper from Derby Works. The degree to which Fowler involved himself with the detail remains unclear. As an acknowledged expert in metallurgy he should have taken a special interest in the materials used for the super high pressure system. We have no information whether he did or not.

With hindsight perhaps too much reliance was placed on the German design and materials specification. Whether Frank Pepper had the knowledge or authority to challenge the Superheater Company is also questionable. There seems no evidence that in 1929 there were indications of potential problems with steam at over 1,000 psi separated from a corrosive coal fire by thin mild steel.

Thus was Fowler convinced that the LMS needed to be involved in the race for 'superpower'. He had an enthusiastic partner in the Superheater Company who would carry the greater financial risk and he was conscious of the work being done by the LNER with Yarrows. His proposition to the LMS Board, albeit supported by dubious claims of greater efficiency, had been accepted. There can be no doubt that this was to be Fowler's Fury.

Chapter Five

THE BUILDING OF FURY

Life begins at NBL

Fowler duly signed the order for Fury which was recorded in NBL as:-

"L858 : - Date ordered, Dec. 15,1928: London Midland and Scottish Railway: One 4-6-0 Passenger Engine (No Tender) Royal Scot Class: fitted with High Pressure Boiler in accordance with Superheater Company's design, now on order under D 3745. General Conditions of L.M. & Scottish specification to offer. As per Offer of 26th. ult. & IIth. inst."

As noted previously, in 1929 NBL had seen its profits fall by 97% in four years and was therefore keen to pick up the order from the LMS for the first batch of 50 Scots. This order alone would have stretched NBL but nevertheless, the collaborative LMS-Superheater Company project was awarded to NBL since it was obvious that the new Scot was the only LMS locomotive which could literally provide the basis for the experiment.

The complex, Schmidt boiler was to be fitted to the chassis of a new Scot. The essential difference between this new Scot chassis and the standard type was the high pressure cylinder fitted between the frames. As the locomotive was a compound (technically a semi-compound), this cylinder and its associated controls were a departure from the normal, simple working of the Scots.

Prior to covering the construction of Fury at NBL, it is worthwhile to examine the structure of Fury and how the component parts were to fit together. To do so, *Fig.3:6* in Chapter 3 can be extended to provide a diagrammatic representation of the locomotive, as *Fig.5:1*.

Fig. 5:1 *Extending Fig.3:6 to show how steam from the 3 independent boilers was utilised in Fury. HP and LP refer to the middle, high pressure cylinder and low pressure, outside cylinders. Red tubes represent intermediate high pressure steam; blue tubes represent low pressure, 'exhausted' steam.*

1	*Primary circuit consisting of foundation ring and vertical water tubes.*
2	*Coal fire in fire box.*
3	*Heat shield (brick arch).*
4	*Intermediate pressure steam drum.*
5	*Low pressure "normal" boiler.*
6	*Low pressure steam take-off.*
7	*Exhaust.*
8	*Locomotive chimney.*

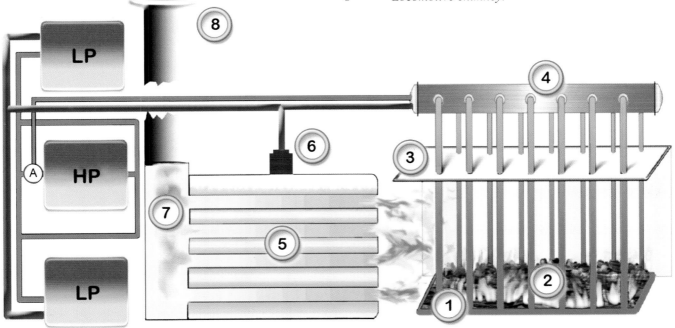

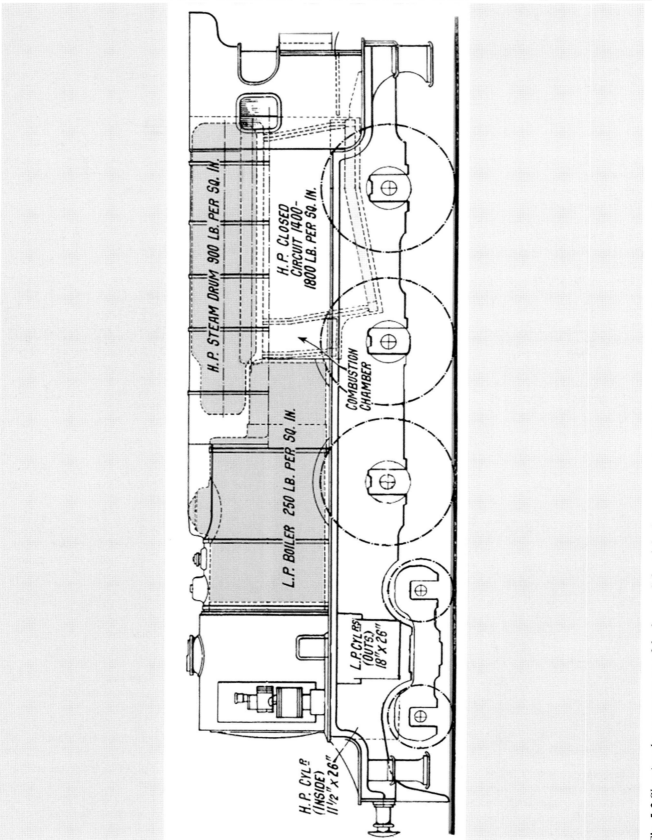

Fig. **5:2** *Showing the arrangement of the 3 main Schmidt boiler components within the constraints of a Scot locomotive outline.*

In *Fig.5:1* above, the source of heat energy is a normal locomotive fire [2] of burning coal, the heat from which raises the temperature of water in the closed coil [1] to around 1,800 pounds per square inch (psi) or 12,400kPa.

The hot flue gases passed into a typical locomotive fire tube boiler [5] where steam was raised at 250 psi (1,723kPa) the exhaust gases [7] then being ejected through the chimney [8].

The closed coil containing the very high pressure steam released most of its heat energy to boil water under pressure in a second chamber – the high pressure steam drum [4] from which steam at about 400psi (2,750kPa) was generated. This steam was taken straight to the single, middle high pressure cylinder of the locomotive and used to supply driving power via the inside crank of the first of the 3 driving axles of the 4-6-0. After the steam in this middle cylinder had been used to drive the piston, it was then mixed with the steam delivered from the 'normal' locomotive fire

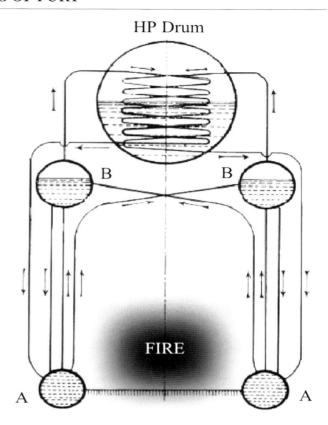

Fig. 5:4 *Diagrammatic vertical section through the smokebox.*

tube boiler at 250 psi and finally delivered to the two outside cylinders that drove the connecting rods which distributed power to all three main axles.

This complicated arrangement meant that Fury was neither a 'simple' nor 'compound' locomotive. Since the whole arrangement was working at very high steam pressure, Fury was technically an "ultra-high pressure, semi-compound steam locomotive".

Of course, the simplistic representation in *Fig.5:1* was much more complex in reality with a diagrammatic arrangement as shown in *Fig.5:2*.

The most obvious external characteristic of Fury would become her two large mixing chambers and Knorr-Bremse pumps inset into either side of the smokebox.

Fig.5:4 Illustrates how water/steam circulated within the closed circuit and thus the heat was transferred to the HP drum. The series of rise and fall pipes between the hollow foundation ring (A) and the equalising drums (B) criss-crossing above the fire constituted the walls of the firebox. Within the HP drum there were the heat exchanger coils *(Fig.5:6)*.

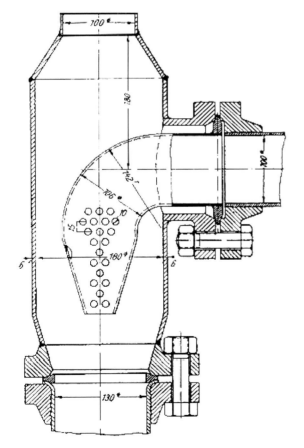

Fig. 5:3 *The mixing chamber, one of which was inset into each side of Fury's smoke box. Their purpose was to mix the superheated LP steam and the exhaust steam from the HP cylinder at about 200 psi. The mixing chambers were claimed by Court to be "simple, efficient and reliable".*

Fig. 5.5 The nickel-steel alloy, HP steam drum as supplied by John Brown of Sheffield and machined at NBL. Its thickness reflects the requirement to withstand 900 psi.

Final machining of the HP steam drum was believed to have been carried out at NBL. The HP drum was insulated from the fire by a suitable bed fixed between the two equalising drums. In addition, the fire box initially had a brick arch installed as was normal locomotive boiler practice.

Fig. 5:6 One of the heat exchanger coils before being fitted inside the HP steam drum. In contrast to the HP steam (above) these coils had to withstand an internal steam pressure of about 1,800 psi.

The drawing office must be commended on their ability to have produced extremely complicated drawings in a short time. Though the copies in the author's possession are undated, they are signed "A. Alston".

The precise date on which NBL began construction is not known, only that it was during November 1928.

The problems confronting The Superheater Company in making the boiler were prodigious. The designed operating pressure for the 'closed loop HP circuit' was extremely high at 1400 to 1800 psi for a tubular system. The tubes themselves within the firebox were naturally exposed to the full heat of the burning coal and its combustion products which might be highly sulphurous depending on the source of coal, giving rise to hot sulphurous and sulphuric acid vapours. Significantly as it turned out, this circuit was only made from ordinary mild steel tube produced to special order by Weldless Tubes Ltd for which, as we have seen from the agreement, Fowler had to have approved.

Court [10] refuted the idea that the boiler was designed by The Superheater Company and stated that all NBL records showed that it was designed by Henschels based upon that used in the earlier German locomotive. This conflicts with Fryer's later belief that the design of the boiler was the work of the Superheater Company, "closely advised" by Henschels [18]. However, the Kassel high pressure locomotive for the German State Railway had a dual high pressure boiler of 853 psi and 205 psi compared to the 1400 to 1800 psi and 900 psi intended for Fury's boiler.
Whatever, this boiler for Fury was certainly pushing the boundaries of knowledge.

Court's assessment of the problems faced at NBL and which

as their projects manager, he would have been acutely aware were summarised by *"The work involved in the construction of the boiler was sufficient to be a challenge to the builders, not only because such a boiler had never before been built in Britain, but because of the manufacturing problems involved – problems which were beyond the orbit of everyday locomotive boiler shop practice."*

Even the third stage of steam generation in a conventional locomotive fire tube boiler was different. Normal locomotive boilers were being pressed to about 175 to 200 psi in the 1920s, so the higher pressure of 250 psi demanded for Fury's fire tube boiler represented further design risk, especially as the overall length of this 3rd stage was less than half that of a normal locomotive fire tube boiler. As a further departure from normal practice, the boiler's outer wrapper was made from nickel steel and the endplates of mild steel.

But it was in the 2nd stage that the most intriguing engineering was introduced. Here the coils *(Figs.5:4 & 5:6)* carrying water vapour at 1400 to 1800 psi would heat surrounding water to produce steam at 800 to 900 psi. The vessel designed to do this - the high pressure drum *(Fig.5:5)* was supplied as a nickel steel forging by John Brown of Sheffield. The forging evidently required some clever machining at NBL and it was eventually subjected to hydraulic testing at "between 1400 and 1800 psi", i.e. rather short of twice its working pressure of 900 psi. At this pressure, there was some deformation of the end door of the high pressure drum, but Court recounted that this was not felt to be a problem, so the drum was passed fit for service.
The Superheater Company blueprints for the boiler exist at the NRM and these show the evident difficulties which presented themselves in shoe-horning the boiler(s) into the Scot chassis *(Fig.5:10)*.

Based on Reed's account [9] Fury was built using the same bogie, chassis, tender as a Scot and with the same wheelbase divisions as a Scot.

But the evidence suggests that Fury's chassis was not in fact a normal Scot chassis. On the official works drawings for Fury the distance from the leading bogie wheel centre to the outer edge of the buffer is shown as 6ft and $^3/_8$ inch whereas the same dimension on the Scots was exactly 5ft. The total length of Fury's frames is shown as 39ft 3in or about one foot longer than those of the Scots. This extra length did not reflect any difference between the wheel centres of Fury and a Scot. An obvious peculiarity of Fury was that the front end of her frame plates was given a concave shape in contrast to all the other Scots.

Components and construction

There are but two published accounts of Fury's build at NBL. The first to be published was in 1971 [19], the second 4 years later [10]. The first account is anonymous but since the wording is almost identical to the second written by Court, either he wrote both or less likely, he copied the earlier account of another author.

The magazine *Model Engineer* had begun a new live-steam model construction series by Martin Evans on Fury and another typical Royal Scot. Provoked by this, John Court submitted two articles in February 1975 and it is these which provide the basis for the account of the build at NBL which follows.

Work on the boiler by the Superheater Company appears to have been carried out alongside the Scot chassis as several images suggest.

Court was of the opinion that accommodating the Schmidt

Fig.5:7 *The front of the frames from Fury (left) and a Scot (right). The curvature and extended length of Fury's frames is evident.*

unit within the frame limits of a Scot "*was a really brilliant piece of design*" and that the manufacturing problems encountered were "*beyond the orbit of everyday locomotive boiler shop practice*" [10].

The third steam raising element – the more normal fire tube boiler – provided steam at 250 psi for the two LP cylinders and in addition, it provided purer water to the HP boiler – the HP steam drum. This feed-water was found to contain only fine suspended particles which did not cause scale or reduction in heat transfer.

We may consider the construction sequence of Fury in terms of:-

1st   The HP drum
2nd   The closed ultra-HP circuit foundation ring
3rd   The LP, fire tube boiler and smokebox
4th   Building the complete locomotive
5th   The cab controls
6th   Painting
7th   Initial steaming

Fig. 5:8 *Stand on which the boiler was to be built.*

Fig. 5:9 *20. Nickel-steel alloy drum in place on erecting stand with four supports each side. One of the lower mixing chambers or 'equalising drums' is below, inside the four supports.*

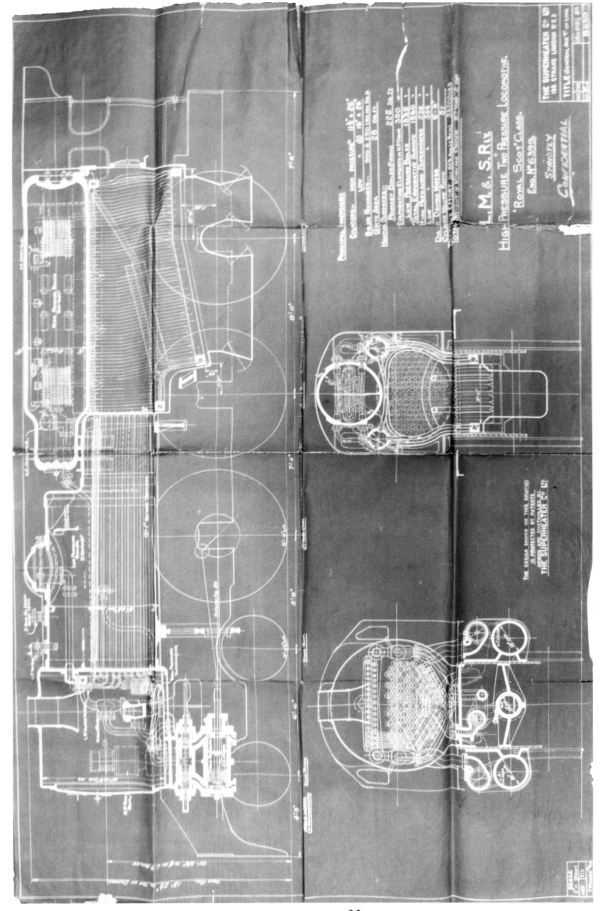

Fig. 5:10 *One of three original blueprints prepared by the Superheater Company. Note the added "STRICTLY CONFIDENTIAL". (Reproduced by kind permission of the National Railway Museum.)*

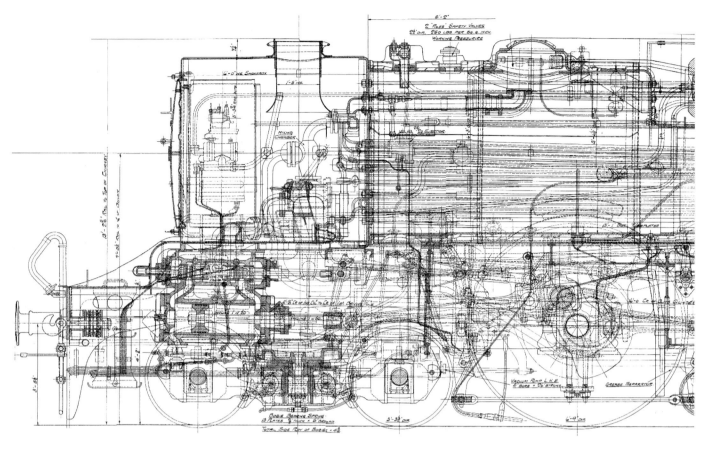

Fig. 5:11 *Reproduction of front section of G.A. Drawing of Fury produced by "A. Alston, N.B. Loco Co Ltd Glasgow". (National Archives of Scotland/Mitchell Library)*

The closed ultra-HP circuit foundation ring.

This comprised, from bottom to top, the hollow foundation ring, the rise and fall tubes surrounding the fire, the two equalising drums and the heat exchanger coils *(Fig.5:4)*.

Returning again to Court's account, to which we must make frequent reference, a significant problem was presented in the fabrication of the hollow foundation ring. He states it was *"finally made from four forgings"* implying that there had been previous unsuccessful attempts.

This is not surprising given that a rectangular section was needed and that this was not in one plane either. In a normal fire tube boiler, the foundation ring is solid and covered by water on one side as it is an integral part of the whole fire box. For Fury, fabrication was much more complicated and evidently *"demanded some really fine workmanship. This applied particularly to the holes for the tubes and thimbles, the edge preparation prior to welding and the actual welding. When completed the unit successfully withstood a test pressure of 2,400 psi."* [10].

With the ultra HP closed circuit operating at 1800 psi hydraulic testing of its integrity was of critical importance.

Fig. 5:12 *Four elements of the foundation ring clamped to a jig and prepared for welding at the four intersections.*

Fig. 5:13 Left, close-up view of the rear portion showing the comparatively small circular joints to be welded. Right, the completed foundation ring, welded, gap-filled and ready for the next stage.

The LP boiler fed water to the HP steam drum via Knorr-Bremse pumps and in turn received its feed water from injectors; one operated from live steam, the other exhaust steam. No steam injector available then or now would supply water to the HP drum given its high internal pressure.

From a cold start, the ultra-HP circuit would obviously create steam from the HP drum much faster than the flue gas heated LP boiler. To avoid this excess steam being wasted while the LP boiler came to pressure, an intercepting valve was fitted to divert this HP steam into the LP boiler.

In addition to the Knorr-Bremse pumps from Germany, most of Fury's boiler fittings and feed pumps came from there also. Apparently, some of them were far from trouble-free for the Superheater Company's fitters.

No descriptions or images are available of the procedure for bending and welding of the tubes which connected the foundation ring to the equalising drums. From later reports, it is known that these tubes were a little more than 2 inch inside diameter with a nominal wall thickness of just 3/16 inch. The tubes were mild steel and German reports [20] had stated that the steam within the tubes would be at about 485° C of superheat. Aware that these tubes would be adjacent to

Fig. 5:14 The LP fire tube boiler shell in position on the frames in November 1929, the bracket to hold the forward part of the HP drum has been fitted.

the fierce fire with all its combustion products it is perhaps surprising that such material was chosen by the Superheater Company and furthermore approved by Fowler.

In order to appreciate how the rise and fall tubes in the ultra-HP circuit were connected to the foundation ring and surrounded the fire, the following picture is worthy of study. Here, the photographer is looking into the 'fire space' towards the front of the fire box. The round gap at the far end, where the tubes are bent, is the hole through which the fireman would shovel coal. The exposed nature of the tubes to flying coal is clear! The two converging pipes in the centre are the supports for the brick arch *(Fig.5:15 below)*

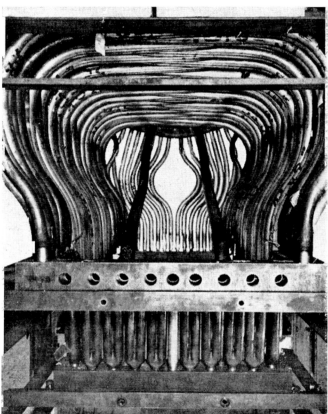

Above - Fig. 5:15

Opposite column - Fig. 5:16
Comparison of smoke boxes: Fury (top), normal Scot (bottom). Was Fury's the original 'plumber's nightmare'?

Fig. 5:17 This photograph shows the nearly completed entire HP system on jacks and either ready to be placed on the chassis or just removed after a trial installation. One cannot help but be struck by the irregular tube bending that had been done. (National Archives of Scotland/Mitchell Library)

Building the complete locomotive

At the beginning of November 1929, with the LP boiler in position on the main frames, Court commented that the nearly finished HP section was placed in position temporarily while wheeling took place. This observation leads to some difficulty in sequencing the NBL photographs at this point. There are several images taken about this time some showing the locomotive with the boiler or boilers *in situ* but with and without driving wheels. Moreover, in one picture the cab sides are in place. It would not be surprising that several attempts at positioning the boilers occurred given the challenges presented.

Several official photographs of Fury's construction at NBL exist, though some originals are thought to have been

removed by Court when NBL closed down in 1962. (John Court then became deputy editor of the *Railway Magazine* for a while after which those photographs have not reappeared).

This author has long been puzzled by some of these photographs because there seems no logical sequence to them. Several other authors, including Court, have reproduced these images in their articles but have merely annotated them with descriptions of what they believe is being done. However there is good evidence that those simple descriptions were incorrect.

The problem can be illustrated by study of 5 particular photographs:-

Above - Fig. 5:18 Photograph 1. This picture reveals several interesting features. As Court had recorded, it appears to show a "nearly finished HP section" being lowered into position after wheels had been fitted. But is this really an installation or in fact removal? The HP boiler erecting frame is still present at the far side of the locomotive and fixed to the wall of the erecting shop in front of the locomotive is a board bearing among other symbols, "L858" which was the NBL order number. It also bears "6399" but the LMS had not assigned this number early in the build. A great deal of the pipe work has been installed but no pistons are evident. The cab side bears a faint, chalked "DO NOT TOUCH". (National Archives of Scotland/Mitchell Library)

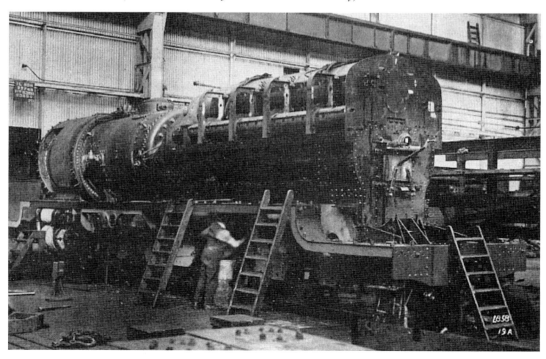

Above - Fig. 5:20 *The third picture (Photograph 3) offers no immediate solution to this puzzle. Here the HP boiler can be seen on its erecting frame but by now the pistons look to have been fitted and therefore the picture has been taken after the first one of these three. Two further pictures just compound the problem of understanding what might have been done and in what sequence.*

Opposite bottom - Fig. 5:19 *Photograph 2. This poor quality image shows the entire HP and LP boilers installed and the framework for cleading already in place. The backhead is well advanced with fire doors fitted. However when compared to Photograph 1, parts of the locomotive are nothing like so far advanced. Close examination suggests that the leading driving wheels are in place but the painter is working on the frames to the rear of this axle and no wheels are covering his work. No cab sides are fitted so unless they and the middle & trailing axles had been removed after the first picture – surely highly unlikely – it would appear photograph 2 predates the first. This raises the possibility that the complete HP system had to be removed for some reason at a late stage in the build. (National Archives of Scotland/Mitchell Library)*

L858-32

Fig. 5:21 Here, in a wider view of Fig. 5:17, Photograph 4 might be thought was taken immediately after or immediately before photograph 1 where the 3 fitters are apparently installing or removing the HP boiler. But this is clearly not the case because it shows the HP drum to have its end caps in place, plugs in the foundation ring and elsewhere and tubes connecting the equalising drums to the steam drum which do not appear in Photograph 1. Disconnected pipes can be seen sticking up from the engine and the connecting rods are now in place. (National Archives of Scotland/Mitchell Library)

The final photograph (5) [Fig, 5:22 opposite top] in this short sequence shows the erecting shed at Hyde Park and Fury can just be seen at the far end. By now the cab has been given the 6399 number, the Fury name plate and significantly, the small brass plaque of the first Fury locomotive can be seen. The partly dismantled HP boiler on its erecting stand has been moved from its position in photograph 3 and yet no connecting rods appear on the wheels.

The puzzle of these photographs may thus be explained. Photograph 4 showing Fury, minus her HP boiler, must definitely be after the Carstairs failure. The driving rods would have been removed in order to tow her back to NBL for repairs but are now replaced. Some of the other photographs, e.g. number 3, may therefore be of this same period where the entire HP system had to be removed for replacement of the burst tube and other significant modifications.

Enlargement of Fury in Photograph 5. The Fury nameplate and small brass plaque can just be made out to the left of the image.

Fig. 5:22
Photograph 5
(National Archives
of Scotland/Mitchell
Library)

The Railway Magazine in early 1929 carried an article in the flowery language of the day which explained the origin of these plaques:-

"SIR HENRY FOWLER, K.B.E., Chief Mechanical Engineer, London Midland & Scottish Railway, has hit upon the happy idea of further perpetuating locomotive history by the addition of brass plates bearing an imprint of one or other of the early locomotives to engines of the "Royal Scot" class bearing the same names. . . . . Several other pioneer locomotives, including Sans Pareil , Novelty, Liverpool and others, have been dealt with in a similar fashion, and perhaps no better or more convenient manner of marking the enormous difference between the original engines, and the modern products bearing the same names, could have been devised. Very considerable interest is aroused among passengers, whose notice is thus attracted"

Fury is mentioned in the article but this of course referred to

locomotive number 6138 which was later renamed "The London Irish Rifleman ". As described earlier in the Introduction, 6138's nameplates were subsequently assigned to 6399 during the latter stages of her build at NBL. However the small brass plaques of the 1831 Fury were not put in place until she was taken from the works in December 1929.

Above - Fig. 5:23 Photograph of original left hand side plaque from Fury. (Sold at auction for £10,200 in 2011) Reproduced by kind permission of Great Central Railwayana Ltd. www.gcrauctions.co.uk)

Left - Fig. 5:24 The right hand nameplate and (8 x 12 inch) brass plaque as fitted to Fury prior to her delivery to the LMS. (H.N.Twells Collection)

Fig. 5:25 *Two views of the cab controls on Fury The right-hand one bears the official photographer's annotations.* *(National Railway Museum)*

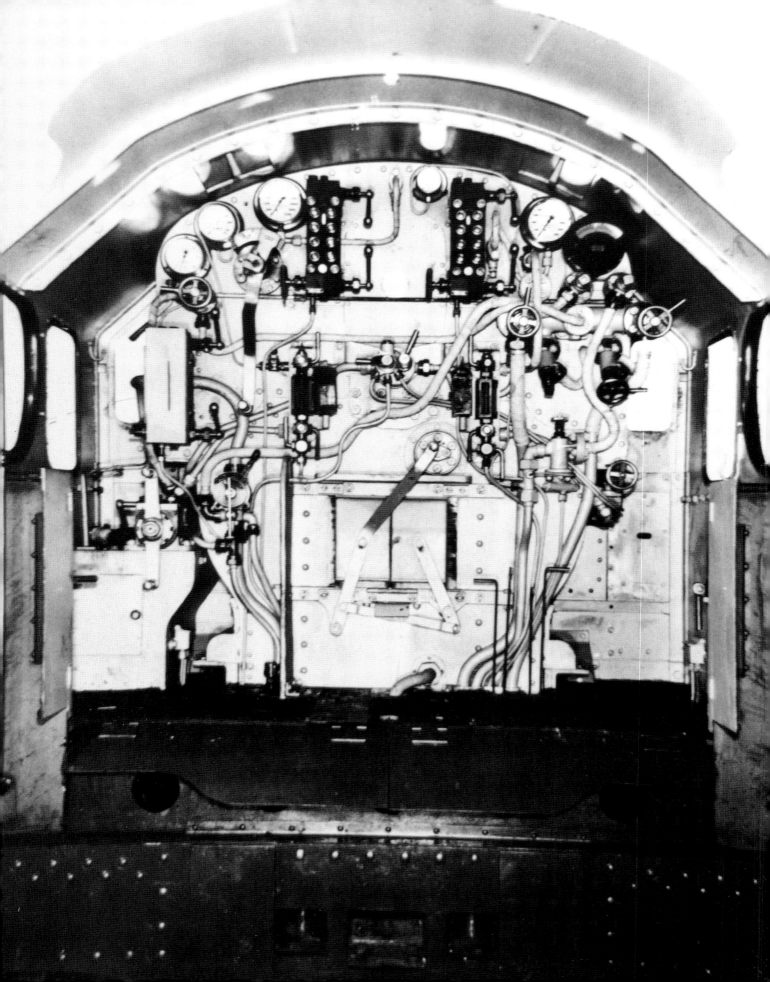

Fig. 5:26 *A comparison of the cabs of Fury (left) and that of a normal Scot (right). There are more than enough controls, gauges, valves etc on a normal locomotive to occupy the driver and fireman when they are watching the road ahead. Driving and firing Fury must have been very taxing for both. (National Railway Museum and National Archives of Scotland/ Mitchell Library)*

Returning to Court's narrative, he wrote:-

"By early December the h.p. unit underwent a preliminary test at 700 p.s.i. and when this was raised to 2000 p.s.i. only a few leaks appeared on some of the larger thimbles and re-expansion provided the cure.
Sir Henry Fowler visited the NBL Hyde Park Works on the morning of the 10th December to see the h.p. section of the boiler on test. After declaring himself completely satisfied he added that it was "a wonderful job". The task of expanding the tubes in position was a particularly onerous one, as a very heavy responsibility rested on those who had to say that the tubes were well and truly expanded in position and that the thimbles could be put in. Once this had been done there was no question of getting at the tube ends again."

Court does not tell us whether the hydraulic test was carried out on the HP system *in situ* on the locomotive. Presumably it was because if Fowler visited NBL on December 10th

1929, which was a Tuesday, he stayed on a few days because Court continues:-

"By the Friday afternoon Fury was ready for steaming tests and the fire was lit at 2.20 p.m. By the evening the locomotive was running on the test bed and, apart from some minor adjustments on the valve gear, piston rod packings, etc.,all was well. Monday, the 6th December, 1929, was a very special day, as it was then that the first official steam tests were carried out, duly witnessed by representatives of the Superheater Co., the L.M.S. and others".

He has clearly confused dates here or a typographical error had been made and the date should be Monday the 16th December.

A photograph held by The Mitchell Library is unfortunately undated but it would seem to be a photographic record of the steaming tests on December 16th. The photograph is of poor quality but with considerable enhancement much more detail of Fury and the assembled group can be seen.

Fig. 5:27 Fury in steam on December 16th 1929 during Fowler's visit to Hyde Park Works. Court wrote that these were all officials of The Superheater Company. However another source states that Fowler is wearing a light coloured trilby hat and is standing below the cab window. Fury now has her name plate affixed to the splasher and the cleading is unfinished. The cab side shows the same markings as the board where she was built (L858, 6399 etc). (National Archives of Scotland/Mitchell Library)

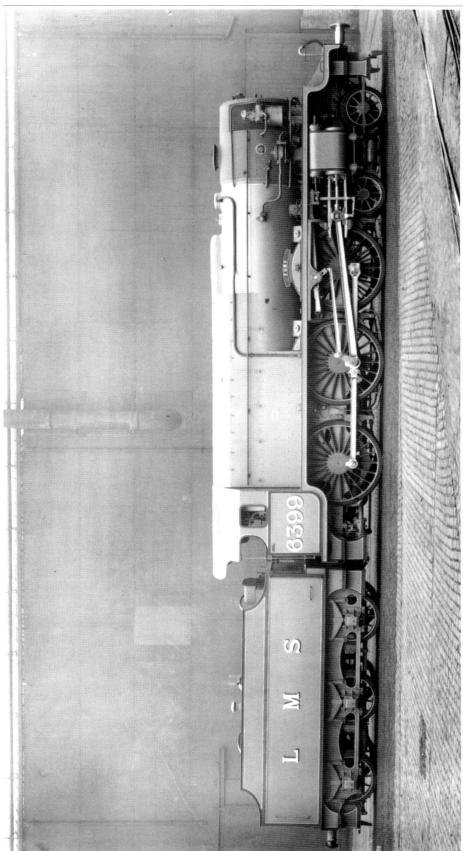

Even with the speed that NBL could operate, it was a tremendous achievement to have assembled a nearly complete and very complex locomotive in a little over one week!

Apparently there were some problems with the regulator when the boiler pressure rose above 500 psi and by the Tuesday of the next week all the minor problems had been corrected, at least temporarily.

Court told the story, often reproduced since, that on the Tuesday when the HP boiler had reached 900 psi the safety valve lifted "with a report like a field gun" and everyone ran for cover. Not really surprising as anyone who has stood next to a locomotive when the safety valve lifts from a pressure a quarter of that can testify!

The final stages of the build seem to have involved rectifying recurring problems with the HP boiler and its ancillary fittings which had been of German origin. The regulator had to control steam from both the 900 psi HP boiler and the 250 psi LP (fire tube) boiler. Court recounts that its valve seats were reground many times before an effective seal was produced.

Yet within only a couple more weeks, Fury had been painted in shop grey for numerous official photographs and was later moved the short distance to the Polmadie running shed.

Fig. 5:28 *Fury painted in shop grey at NBL in early February 1930 A comparatively rare shot of her full right-hand side. The small brass plaque of the first Fury had not yet been fitted. A standard "Fowler" tender of 3,500 gallon water and 5 ½ ton coal capacities had been assigned. The 'LMS Tender History Card' suggests this was tender number 3923 but doubt exists. The oval plate on the side of the firebox was worded. "The Superheater Co. Ltd., Bush House, Aldwych, London. Schmidt high pressure two pressure loco boiler. (National Archives of Scotland/Mitchell Library)*

Above - Fig. 5:29 *In steam this time, an image often reported to show Sir Henry Fowler leaning out the cab. However, this is incorrect – see the following picture and notes. (National Archives of Scotland/ Mitchell Library)*

Left - Fig. 5:30 *Enlargement of previous photograph which shows it is Mrs Stenning and unknown person leaning from the cab side.*

Note on those present - *The image bears little resemblance to Henry Fowler. Others have claimed a similarity to Nigel Gresley but it is highly improbable that it was him. His wife had died in August of that year following which he and his daughter went to Canada on holiday. Anyway, his presence at NBL would certainly have been recorded !*

Right - Fig. 5:31 According to Court [40], this picture shows "centre, Col. H. A. Stenning, OBE Director of the Superheater Company and on his right, Mrs Stenning. The source of the information is "The Locomotive" of 15th November, 1934, and "the curriculum vitae of Col. Stenning, which appeared on p.350 - the eve of his retirement together with a photograph. The identity of the man on the right of the picture is unknown although it has been claimed to be Fowler. It is doubtful if Fowler and Col. Stenning were ever at the NBL works at the same time, as the recorded dates of their visits were separated by a gap of four days".

Figs. 5:32 (above) and 5:33 (overleaf) Two images from the original glass negatives at The Mitchell Library. Both had deteriorated with many marks and scratches which have been removed by the author. They are perhaps the most detailed pictures of Fury known. (National Archives of Scotland/Mitchell Library)

THE RAILWAY GAZETTE

THE RAILWAY GAZETTE.	JANUARY 3, 1930.

THE NEW "ROYAL SCOT" HIGH-PRESSURE LOCOMOTIVE, L.M.S.R.

Design incorporates 900 and 250 lb. per sq. in., Double-pressure Boiler and Three Cylinders operating on the Compound Principle.

On page 1011 of *The Railway Gazette*, dated December 27, 1929, there appeared a general description of the new high-pressure three-cylinder compound locomotive, recently completed at the works of the North British Locomotive Company, Glasgow, for the L.M.S. Railway. This information is supplemented by the photographs and drawing reproduced herewith. The engine, in its general aspects, corresponds to the "Royal Scot" class, differing therefrom in possessing a special type of boiler, incorporating a double-pressure system of 900 and 250 lb. per sq. in., as developed by the Superheater Co. Ltd., of Bush House, Aldwych, W.C.2. This system in its general principles has already had fairly extended trials on a 4-6-0 type locomotive belonging to the German railways, the engine having been converted from a standard type, with ordinary boiler, at the works of Henschel & Sohn, Kassel.

The main difference between the previous *Royal Scot* locomotive and the new type, apart from the boiler, is in the fact that in the latter case, the cylinders operate on the compound, instead of the single-expansion, system. This change secures the advantageous use of very high-pressure steam by increasing the range of steam expansion, thus getting more work out of the steam before final exhaust takes place. The high-pressure cylinder between the frames has a diameter of 11½ in., whilst the low-pressure cylinders outside each measure 18 in. in diameter, a common piston stroke of 26 in. being employed. As compared with this, the standard engine has three 18 in. by 26 in. single-expansion cylinders, using steam at 250 lb. per sq. in. The adhesion weight in the previous

design was 62 tons 10 cwt., this being increased in the new engine to an estimated total of 63 tons 2 cwt. The new boiler doubtless weighs more than the original one, and this would have the effect of increasing the weight on the coupled wheels. The weight carried by the leading bogie in the *Royal Scot* standard engine is 22 tons 8 cwt.; this is increased to 24 tons (estimated) in the new design. The estimated weights refer to the engine in working order, in both cases.

A similar comparison of the respective figures for tractive force shows that the earlier locomotives each developed 33,150 lb., and here again there is an increase of a moderate character, the figure being 33,200 lb. for the new engine.

The standard *Royal Scot*, in working order, without tender, weighs 84 tons 8 cwt., whilst the high-pressure type, according to the estimated weights, will turn the scale at 87 tons 2 cwt. Whereas the previous maximum weight on any axle was 20 tons 18 cwt., the maximum again expressed in approximate terms is now 21 tons 2 cwt., this being the load placed upon each of the driving coupled axles, whilst the trailing wheels, similarly calculated, now carry 20 tons 18 cwt., as compared with the 20 tons 14 cwt. of the previous design.

The locomotive, which has been built under the supervision of Sir Henry Fowler, K.B.E., Chief Mechanical Engineer, L.M.S.R., has been introduced experimentally for the purpose of working the heaviest main-line express trains and, according to report, it is intended to test it later on non-stop runs between Glasgow and London.

Fig. 5:34 The second report on Fury in The Railway Gazette and showing that the LMS had revealed much data on Fury in December of 1929.

Painted Fury

Over the years controversy has arisen over whether Fury was ever painted in full LMS crimson lake livery. Holt [21] wrote an informative article on the subject in which he analysed the 'pros and cons'. He concluded that at some point, she had certainly been given the full crimson lake livery.

It was common practice at that time for newly built, first of a series, engines to be painted in shop grey (or incorrectly "photographic" grey). The official photographs of such locomotives were taken with a plate camera using black & white emulsion on a glass negative. Shop grey paint therefore was particularly useful in showing contrast and detail with emulsions of that period. In Figs.5:33 & 5:34 the front buffer beam has no lining out whereas the bogie wheels have been lined but the driving wheels possibly not.

Other areas have obviously been lined such as on the running boards, steps and cylinder cleading. Shortly after these images were taken, a further series of photographs were taken whilst Fury was still at NBL but now, the front buffer beam has been lined. Reed [9] reports that Fury was "painted red" at Hyde Park.

The Illustrated History of British Steam Railways contains a picture of Fury [46]. Neither the source nor date is given but it was clearly taken at NBL whilst Fury was very obviously still in shop grey paint. Fowler would appear to have signed the glass negative for his signature is in white and therefore he may have done so at NBL on or about December 16th 1929. It shows the brass plaque has been fitted. If this is correct, it suggests that Fury was given crimson lake livery between then and early February when handed over to the LMS.

Fig. 5:35 Fury in steam at NBL but perhaps giving the appearance of still being in shop grey despite the lining on the buffer beam which would otherwise suggest she had been painted in crimson lake. It is just another example of the uncertainties in establishing when, or as some maintain if, full LMS livery was applied.

Fig. 5:36 Fury again in steam at NBL, front buffer beam lined and brass plaques of original 1831 Fury are fitted. This author believes that all images from this point onwards are almost certainly in crimson lake livery.

THE BUILDING OF FURY

Opposite top - Fig. 5:37 Fury at Hyde Park Works being closely examined (H.N. Twells collection).

Opposite bottom - This photograph (Fig. 5:38) is as the one above at Hyde Park Works on February 6th 1930 and from a higher vantage point. The likelihood of correct LMS livery now having been applied is apparent. (Getty Archive G957)

Above - Fig. 5:39 The Yarrow water tube boiler for LNER 10000, the "Hush hush". Though simpler that the Schmidt type used in Fury and only designed for a maximum pressure of 450 psi – the basic similarities are clear

Bottom - Fig. 5:40 A poor original much enhanced, Fury at Hyde Park Works looking ready to move off.

Fig. 5:41 Taken at the same time as Fig.5:40 but presumably rejected for publicity purposes because of poor quality. A man poses here with oil can as though lubricating a coupling rod bearing. It will have been taken on February 6th or 7th 1930, the latter being the day on which Fury was formally handed over to the LMS. She appears immaculate and must surely be in full crimson lake livery.

Fig. 5:42 *Reportedly taken on February 7th 1930. The rear of what was a somewhat ill-informed press image reported, "On trial at Glasgow having been delivered to the LMS yesterday, Britain's latest locomotive for speed supremacy". If only ! The idea of improved efficiency would not sell newspapers - the conquest of speed probably would. (Getty Archive G960)*

Above - Fig. 5:43 *Taken after Fig.5:35 and showing - as in the previous image – the poor combustion which was to affect Fury during her trials from Derby.*

Right - Fig.5: 44 *Leaving the works following which many more static photographs were taken in addition to the short Gaumont British Pathe film (see reference26).*

Fury was handed over to the LMS whilst she was still at NBL and since NBL were contracted to provide Scot locomotives in LMS livery, there is no evidence that Fury was treated differently. Though no conclusive proof, either written or photographic exists of Fury being painted in crimson lake, the case is strong that she was.

Movement at NBL

Fury was 'out shopped' from the Hyde Park Works at NBL on February 6th 1930, just over 13 months since construction began of *"a locomotive of extraordinary complexity"*[10]. The routine at NBL was for locomotives to be moved from their works to the Polmadie Running Shed. Most, but not all

LMS and LNER (and BR) locomotives built by the NBL were erected at Queen's Park Works because of this easy access to a main line. LMS locos (like the Jubilees and 2-6-4 tanks) were towed to Polmadie shed, a short distance away, on delivery. Fury however went from Hyde Park Works to the Polmadie Shed under her own steam[22].

The next day, February 7th, she was formally handed over to the LMS.

The LMS had first released details of their new project in late 1929[23], with the noted railway scribe Cecil J. Allen subsequently reporting in his regular column[ibid] :-

". . . . It is highly interesting to note that the London

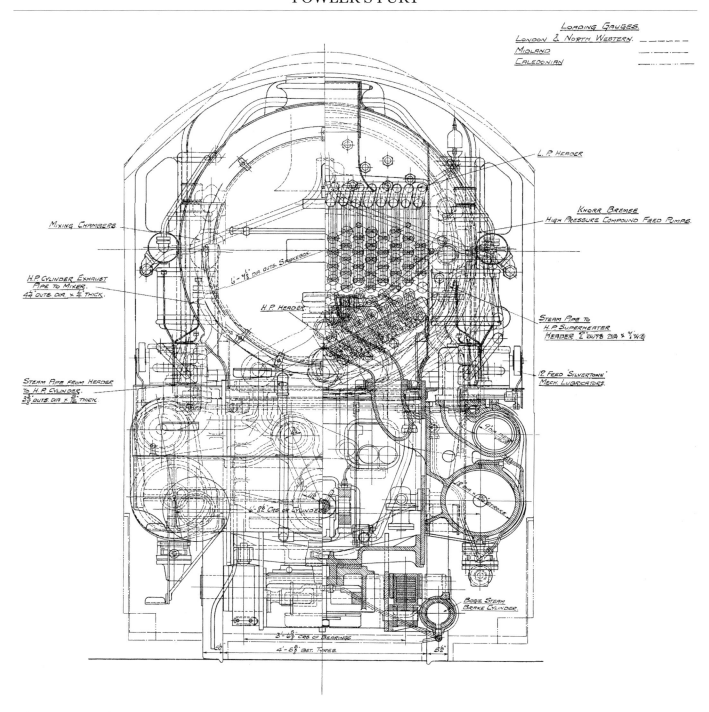

Fig. 5:45 *Reproduction of transverse section of G.A. Drawing of Fury produced by "A. Alston, N.B. Loco Co Ltd Glasgow". (Mitchell Library). This scanned drawing is taken from genuine copies of NBL material, rather than 'Set Tracings' sent to the LMS at Derby at the conclusion of a contract. They carry the correct NBL title blocks and contract number in the top right.*

Opposite bottom - *The 'Mecanno' version. (XVII. 7. 536. July 1932.)*

Midland & Scottish Railway Company is having built by the North British Locomotive Company a 4-6-0 locomotive of this type, to work as a three-cylinder compound at these pressures, but conforming otherwise in general proportions with the Royal Scot against which it is to be tested."

However once Fowler had visited NBL on December 10th 1929 to pronounce his "satisfaction", the LMS publicity department elatedly began to trumpet their new locomotive. Full details of Fury with pictures of her construction began to appear.

In February 1930 *The Railway Engineer* carried a short but comprehensive article [24].

The Railway Magazine's February edition announced "The experimental high-pressure locomotive, designed by *(sic)* Sir Henry Fowler. K,B,E,........has now been completed"[27].

From one extreme to the other, the new locomotive was inspiring articles in boys' magazines. Men and boys were encouraged to make Fury models in Meccano with Frank Hornby gleefully noting "...not only in this country but all over the world" [25].

The LMS persuaded Gaumont Graphic Newsreel to come to NBL and film Fury as she steamed *en route* from Hyde Parks Works to Polmadie but whether this disjointed and silent film was ever shown on cinema newsreels is not known. (The 57 second clip can be seen on the ITN Source website [26]).

Sadly, it was to prove a short-lived period of elation for the LMS.

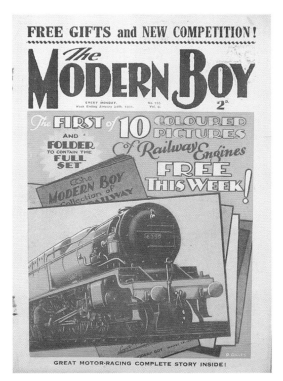

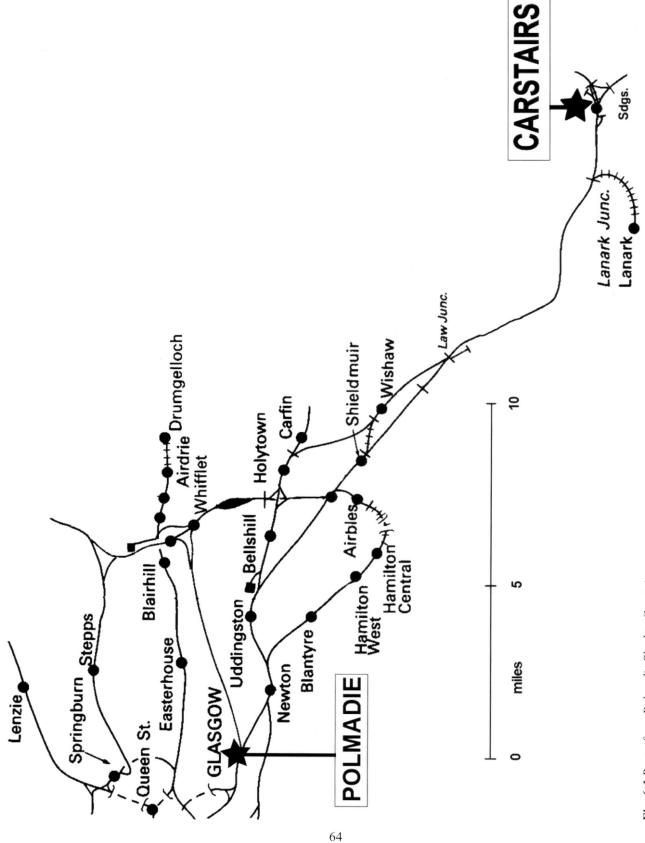

Fig..6:1 Route from Polmadie Shed to Carstairs.

Chapter Six

CARSTAIRS

Sequence of events, testimonies, and court enquiry, conclusions and LMS investigations

Under the terms of the agreement [28] between the Superheater Company and the LMS, once the Railway Company took over Fury both companies were jointly responsible for the "tests and trials" and these were to be completed within 6 months of the handover. Clause 7 of the agreement stated "that these tests and trials shall be comprehensive and shall include indicating, dynamometer car tests and all other usual locomotive tests". Clearly the LMS accepted the dominant role during this period and Clause 7 merely invited the Superheater Company "if it so desires" to arrange for its engineers to be present.

Conscious of the time pressures as well as their rival LNER's first running on December 12th of their own experimental locomotive (the so called "hush hush"), the LMS must have been anxious to press ahead with testing as soon as possible. Clause 8 of the agreement was explicit:-

"The Railway Company, having completed all these tests and trials to the joint satisfaction of the Railway Company and the Superheater Company, shall, without delay, place the locomotive in traffic in a suitable district and on suitable work for the purpose of carrying out traffic tests in accordance with its usual custom in testing locomotives of a new design".

In terms of these two clauses in the agreement, there is some uncertainty as to what stage had been reached when Fury was moved from Hyde Park to Polmadie, ready for main line running. Court wrote that the first official steam tests began on December 6th 1929. The move from Hyde Park to Polmadie does not appear to have involved any particular testing of Fury. It would seem therefore that on February 6th 1930, the first real testing under clause 7 was to commence on main line track.

The driver had been allocated at the end of December. He was Donald Hall from the Polmadie Shed. Hall was aged 59 and an experienced driver with 2 ½ years of working the Scots from Glasgow.

Driver Hall and his fireman, Donald Blair had been relieved of normal duties in mid January to spend a meagre 2 days at Hyde Park Works familiarising themselves with the complexities of Fury.

Both were evidently conscientious men and they quickly concluded that they needed more experience of the locomotive. It was especially naïve or foolhardy of the LMS to have believed those 2 days with a static Fury was remotely adequate for familiarisation with such a complicated locomotive. As a result both men were allowed to spend a further 4 days at Hyde Park in early February; the second two of which they practised moving Fury up and down the works' sidings.

After these sessions, driver Hall pronounced himself familiar with the handling of the engine.

During these familiarisation runs Hall and Blair were accompanied by Francis Pepper. He was the young engineer and experimental draughtsman from the CME's Department at Derby. Pepper played an important part in Fury's development, having been appointed the previous June to supervise Fury's construction at NBL. He had also been instructed to supervise the testing which would be carried out once Fury had been handed over to the LMS Traffic Department

On February 6th in the late afternoon and therefore in darkness, the driver, fireman and Pepper took Fury from Hyde Park to Polmadie arriving there just under 2 hours later. As the distance between Springburn and Polmadie was about 5 miles, they must have either encountered numerous signal stops or drove at a slow walking pace. Even so, Driver Hall described it as a successful run. On arrival, Driver Hall made to shed the engine when the joint in the right hand pump discharge chamber blew. Pepper arranged for repairs to be carried out the next day (Saturday), ready for the main line testing to begin on the following Monday morning.

Early on the morning of Monday, February 10th the crew clocked in at 7.00 and Blair, the fireman got ready to build the fire. On the previous Friday, Pepper had instructed the shed that the boilers should be filled ready. But as part of his pre-lighting routine, when Blair checked the sight glasses, he observed that the low and intermediate pressure boilers showed correct levels whereas he had difficulty determining the water level in the closed (ultra high pressure) circuit. Nevertheless, both Driver Hall and Francis Pepper instructed Blair that the level was sufficient for him to build the fire.

Pressure was slow to rise and in desperation at some point a connection was made to an adjacent locomotive and steam was bled from this engine to the low pressure boiler of Fury via her ejector steam pipe.

Three hours and twenty minutes after Hall and Blair arrived at Fury she finally had sufficient steam to leave the shed.

The plan was for Fury to run light from Polmadie to Carstairs where she would be turned on the triangle before returning to Polmadie.

On the footplate would be Driver Hall, Fireman Blair, Francis Pepper the Derby engineer/draughtsman and Lewis Schofield from the Superheater Company (not Louis Schofield as often recorded).

The run down from Polmadie was fairly uneventful but slow, with just one short stop at Hamilton Palace Colliery signal box to correct a blowing drain cock on the high pressure cylinder. This was after running for just over 7 miles.

As they approached Carstairs, Driver Hall slowed Fury and all water gauges were checked. The fireman opened the firebox doors and noted the fire was low but as they were due to stop at Carstairs, he checked with Pepper and they agreed to wait until they had stopped at the station before rebuilding the fire. The pressures in the closed circuit and two boilers were noted as "about 1000, 800 and 250 psi" respectively.

As they approached the platform ramp, Hall had slowed Fury to about 6 mph and was looking out of his side of the cab.

The firebox doors had been left open.

Just before coming to a halt alongside the platform at Carstairs there was a huge explosion.

One of the tubes in the ultra-high pressure circuit had split open and the escaping steam blew the contents of the firebox out of the open firebox doors from where they rebounded off the front of the tender and covered the footplate with burning coal.

Colonel Stenning said later that he estimated the escape of steam lasted about 3 to 3½ seconds and would have been initially about 290° C (550° F). Some 120 gallons of water had been expelled in those 3 seconds.

Lewis Schofield took the full force of the steam and the expelled burning coals as he happened to be standing closest to the open firebox doors.

Driver Hall stayed at the controls despite the fact that his clothing was on fire. Fireman Blair decided to jump – exiting through the opening on the right of the cab and injuring himself as he hit the ground.

With his overalls also on fire, Francis Pepper grabbed the roof edge of the cab and pulled himself clear of the footplate and hung there, outside the engine until it was brought to a stop by the driver.

Pepper then got down and tried to drag the unfortunate Lewis Schofield from the footplate but found one of his legs to be trapped. With help from Driver Hall and station staff, they carried him off the footplate still covered with burning coal, to the platform where the station staff immediately rushed to attend him.

Driver Hall, once his burning clothes were extinguished and his dungarees removed, had the presence of mind to put on the injector and using the coal dust suppression hose, put out the burning coals on the footplate. He then dropped the grate and what remained of the fire fell into the ashpan.

Despite sustaining a burned wrist, the dutiful Donald Hall stayed with Fury and even noted that the low pressure boiler showed 200 psi and the high pressure boiler 700 psi.

The impact of the violent explosion and then witnessing the horrific injuries to Lewis Schofield would have been very traumatic for Hall and Pepper. But within a short time an engine was brought up to tow Fury to the Carstairs shed and Hall remained with it until made safe. A little later the heroic Driver Hall simply boarded the 13:17 from Carstairs train as a passenger and headed back to Glasgow and presumably Polmadie to report back to work.

Lewis Schofield's injuries and consequential pain must have been excruciating. He received first aid from the Carstairs station staff and Dr Marshall, a local G.P. was summoned. It was quickly decided that he required specialist treatment and a further locomotive was hurriedly brought up to which was attached a single van. This rushed him across from Carstairs to Edinburgh.

The unfortunate man died the following day from his injuries in Edinburgh Royal Infirmary.

There then followed two separate but related enquiries; one to determine the cause of the pipe failure (for immediately after the incident it was apparent a pipe had burst), the second, a fatal accident inquiry, to determine the cause of death of Mr Lewis Schofield.

The public, fatal accident inquiry was to be held on March 21st 1930 by Sheriff Wilson K.C. before a jury at Lanark. The LMS moved fast and commissioned the production of

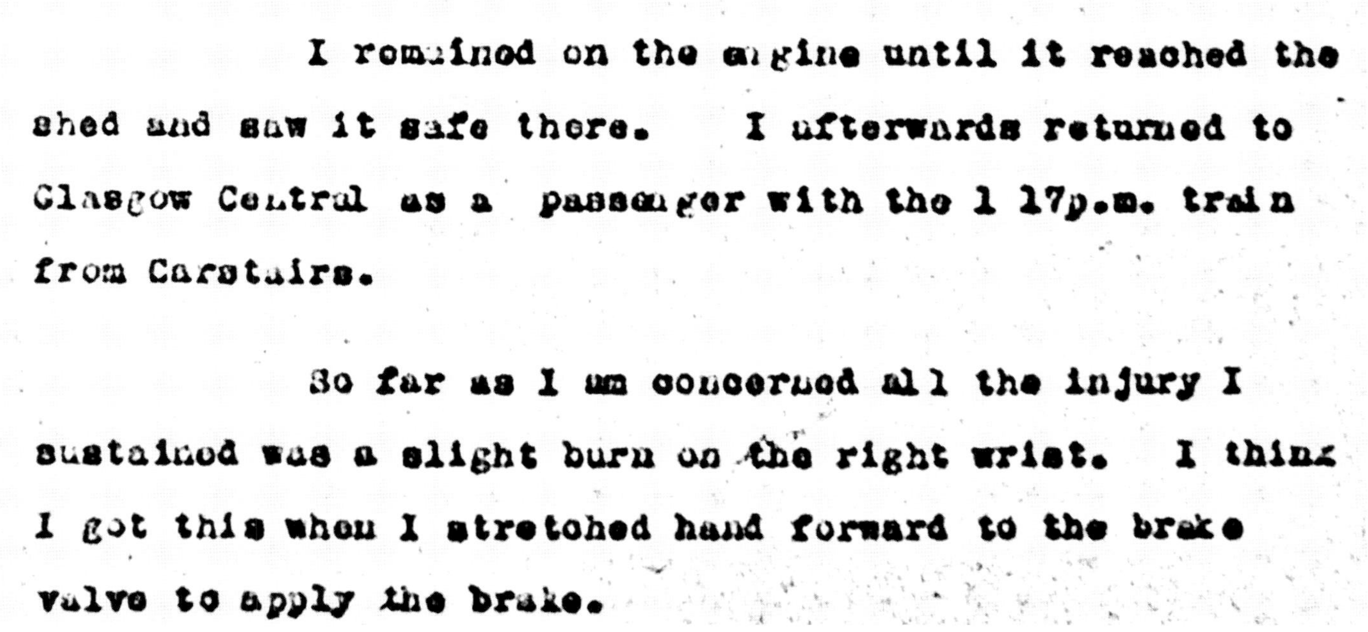

I rem.ined on the engine until it reached the shed and saw it safe there. I afterwards returned to Glasgow Central as a passenger with the 1 17p.m. train from Carstairs.

So far as I am concerned all the injury I sustained was a slight burn on the right wrist. I think I got this when I stretched hand forward to the brake valve to apply the brake.

Fig. 6:2 Driver Donald Hall, the unsung hero at Carstairs, the final part of his submission to the Fatal Accident Inquiry - a prime example of stoicism and understatement. (National Railway Museum)

various drawings and documents by Herbert Chambers, technical assistant and chief draughtsman to Fowler. Two of the drawings showed the boiler and where the tube burst occurred.

These were submitted by James Wilson, the LMS solicitor in Glasgow to the Procurator-Fiscal one week before the inquiry.

At the inquiry, evidence was presented by Driver Hall, Fireman Blair and Francis Pepper.

Francis Pepper opined that although he could not be sure that it alone was the cause of the burst, he had observed a "hair flaw" on the surface of the pipe. Exactly when and how he could have observed this was not recorded. Neither was there any reference to what follow up action he took after noting this "hair flaw". In fact it is difficult to appreciate how Pepper could have noticed this because the failed tube was set well back in the firebox and above the brick arch *(see Fig.6:5)*.

At the inquiry, Thomas Lawson the works manager at Hyde Park told the court that on later inspection, he found the pipe in question was 5.32 inches in diameter and the length of the split was 5½ inches long. But his measurements could not have been correct. Reference to *Fig.6:4* shows that the split was twice as long as the tube diameter. Furthermore *Fig.6:6* reveals that the tubes were just over 2 inches in diameter. Neither Pepper's "hair flaw" nor Lawson's incorrect measurements were challenged in the court.

The LMS had also sent along Herbert Chambers, chief draughtsman from the Derby D.O. His evidence included the information that the tubes had been made by the Weldless Company and in his opinion, their thickness "was quite sufficient to withstand the pressure." [29]

Given their responsibilities, it is strange that nothing is recorded about the role of the "Weldless Company" in the subsequent LMS investigations of the Carstairs incident beyond a single inspection by one of their representatives. This Birmingham company had begun in the 19th C as the Star Tube Co., which later became part of the combine known as Weldless Tubes Ltd. (later Tubes Ltd.). It was acquired in 1929 by I.C.I. and remained in business until 1958. They were a regular supplier of tubes to the LMS and proudly promoted this in their advertising.

The Jury returned a formal verdict of accidental death.

The LMS later paid Mr Schofield's widow compensation in an out of court settlement.

Donald Hall never received any of the praise or reward he undoubtedly deserved for his commendable devotion to duty at Carstairs. Had he not stayed at the controls with his overalls on fire, Fury may have continued to run for some distance since we may assume the regulator was still cracked open.

In the weeks following Carstairs, several letters passed between the LMS lawyers at Euston and Glasgow [33].

ENGINE MISHAP

THE EXPLOSION ON THE "FURY"

INQUIRY INTO DEATH OF TESTING EXPERT

Interesting evidence regarding the construction of the L.M.S. high-pressure locomotive Fury, on which an explosion took place at Carstairs last month on the first long-distance test, was given at the County Buildings, Lanark, yesterday, when an investigation was held into the death of Mr Lewis Schofield, an official of the Super-Heating Co., London, which was associated with the building of the engine. The inquiry was conducted by Sheriff Wilton, K.C., before a jury.

It was stated that the new engine was of German design and was the first of its type to be introduced into this country.

DRIVER'S EVIDENCE

Mr Schofield who resided at 11 South Hamilton Street, Kilmarnock, was travelling on the engine during the running of its first test on February 10, and as a result of the explosion he was so severely scalded by steam and burning coal which escaped from the fire-box of the locomotive that he died the following day in the Glasgow Royal Infirmary.

Donald Hall (58), 762 Rutherglen Road, Glasgow, the driver of the Fury, stated in evidence that the engine worked quite satisfactorily on its run from Glasgow until Carstairs Junction was reached. As the locomotive was proceeding at a slow pace at that point there was a loud explosion, and fire and steam "came all round them on the footplate out of the fire-box." The speed during the journey varied from about 15 to 50 miles an hour. He paid particular attention to the pressure gauges of the engine, and saw that the closed circuit indicated 1000 or 1100lb. of pressure, while the maximum for that circuit was 1400 to 1800lb. The high pressure registered between 700 and 800, and the low pressure 200lb., while the respective maxima were 900 and 250lb.

Following the accident he brought the engine up within a distance of about 50 yards, and then noticed that Mr Schofield was lying on the footplate in a state bordering on collapse. His clothes were smouldering. Mr Schofield, he added, was in such a position as to receive the full force of the rush of steam and coal.

Corroborative evidence was given by Donald Blair (28), 15 Bankhall Street, Govanhill, Glasgow, the fireman, who explained that he managed to escape the full pressure of the steam by jumping on to the station platform.

"HAIR FLAW IN PIPE."

Francis Joseph Pepper (27), a supervising draughtsman in the employment of the L.M.S Railway Co. at Derby, who was a passenger on the engine, said that he had been closely in touch with the designing and building of the engine. He was perfectly satisfied with the running and working of the locomotive prior to the accident. He examined the engine following the explosion and found a burst pipe in the roof of the fire-box. The engine, he said, was of a German pattern, and was the first of its type to be introduced into this country.

He could not form any opinion as to the cause of the accident, but examination revealed that "there was a hair flaw on the surface of the pipe." Asked if it were a defect, he said he could not define it as such. The fracture in the pipe might have been accentuated by the presence of the hair flaw.

PIPE EQUAL TO THE PRESSURE.

Thomas Lawson (49) works manager at the Hydepark Locomotive Works, Springburn, where the engine was built, also spoke to finding the burst in the pipe inside the fire-box after the accident. He explained that the pipe was 5.32in. in thickness, and the length of the burst was approximately 5½in.

Herbert Chambers (45), technical assistant and chief draughtsman at the L.M.S. works, Derby, said that the tubes in the fire-box were made at Wednesfield, in the Birmingham district. The thickness of the fractured tube, he added, was quite sufficient to withstand the pressure.

The jury returned a formal verdict in accordance with the evidence led.

Fig. 6:3 The Glasgow Herald, Saturday March 22nd 1930.

Fig..6:4 *View inside the firebox clearly showing the split tube. From reference to Fig.6:5, the photograph was taken from the firing end of the firebox. When built, Fury was fitted with a brick arch in the firebox – this has possibly been removed here. A smaller replacement was fitted much later. (National Archives of Scotland/Mitchell Library)*

Fowler wrote to them in April of 1930 seeking clarification on the complexities of the agreement between the LMS and the Superheater Company and the contract with NBL. He wanted to know for example, who actually owned Fury at the time of the Carstairs incident? Had it passed over to the LMS or not? The answers would indicate that Fury had not been formally handed over to the LMS by the contractors but was nevertheless 'run by' LMS employees. These were identified as John Keyden, District Locomotive Superintendent, LMS Running Sheds, Polmadie who was in charge of operations and Francis Pepper of the CME's Department in Derby.

Eventually, G.L. Smythe from the Solicitors Office at Euston decided that whatever the complexities of the various agreements "responsibility does lie upon the Railway Company".

Such disputes were to rumble on for several more years eventually coming to an end in July 1934 – about the same time as Fury did likewise.

The Technical Investigation by the LMS.

Immediately after the incident at Carstairs a team must have been sent down from NBL to Fury. Clearly unable to move under her own steam, she would have had to be towed back to Hyde Park by another locomotive. For towing over such a distance her connecting and coupling rods would probably have been removed. Once back in the erecting shop on February 12th the tube was examined *in situ* by a representative of the Weldless Tube Co. following which the entire high pressure system was removed in order to access the burst tube (Possibly the stage shown in Fig. 5:18 Chapter 5.)

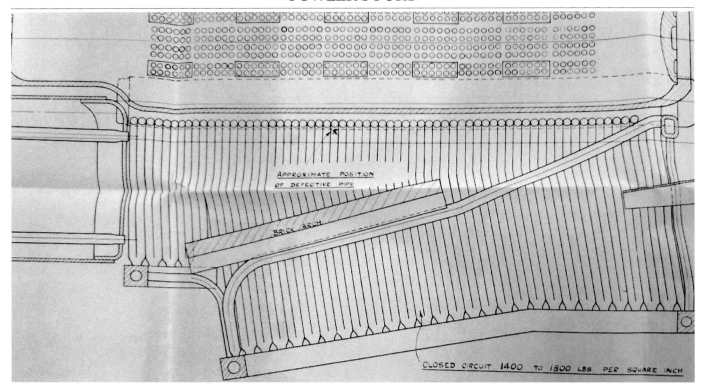

Fig. 6:5 Part of drawing produced by the Derby D.O. and is the clearest picture of where the burst pipe was located in relation to the fire box and brick arch. (National Railway Museum)

Fowler agreed that expert examination of the burst tube was necessary and recognising Sheffield University's close relationship with its steel industry, Professor Lea of their Department of Mechanical Engineering was asked to conduct a thorough study.

Sixsmith[7] records that Dr Frank Smith of the Royal Society and Secretary to the Department of Industrial & Scientific Research was also asked to assist in the investigation, but no

reference to this currently exists in the NRM Archives.

The tube was dispatched to the university and the first internal report was produced on March 27th 1930 by C. Desch of the Department of Applied Science.

This ruled out that the "hair flaw" noted by Pepper was implicated in the bursting. At this stage, prior to microscopic evaluation, it was concluded that the brick arch

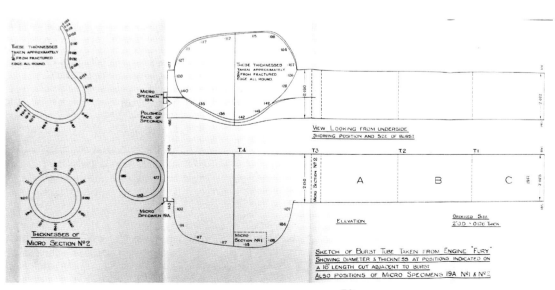

Fig. 6:6 Drawing produced at Sheffield University to show area of burst and where micro specimens were taken for analysis (National Railway Museum)

was directing heat on to this part of the firebox roof and there was insufficient flow of water through the closed circuit, leading to a dry steam pocket on the inside of the tube. Desch did not advocate using thicker tubes but paradoxically suggested they should be as thin as possible consistent with an internal pressure of 1,400 psi.

Meanwhile detailed photomicrographic examination of tube sections continued.

By April 25th Professor Lea was in a position to send a further report to Fowler (but not apparently to the Superheater Company which owned the boiler) and he concluded:-

> "It seems clear, therefore, that the tube which bulged has been exposed for some considerable time to a temperature of at least 650°C, whilst the contact of the flame with the actual surface has produced burning and intercrystalline oxidation. At such a temperature mild steel creeps to a very considerable extent under a stress of 2 tons per square inch."

Quite why Lea referred to "a stress of 2 tons per square inch" is unclear. This represented over twice the working pressure of 1800 psi in the closed circuit. It would have been of more value to give data about creep in mild steel at half that value.

One month later, Lea wrote again to Fowler enclosing photomicrographs but adding little to the earlier communication. He now thought there was evidence the tube had been heated to 800°C and he reiterated Desch's conclusion that a "dry pocket" had been formed inside the tube which led to "creep".[30]

The Sheffield University study was comprehensive but in effect inconclusive and would have provided little or nothing of immediate practical value to the LMS or the Superheater Company.

It should be remembered that Fury's Schmidt type boiler actually belonged to the Superheater Company, not to the LMS. The surviving records however only show exchanges passing between Fowler or his team and Sheffield University.

We have no knowledge of the Superheater Company's response to these reports or what action was taken or proposed to the LMS by them as owners of the boiler. But Sixsmith reproduced a report dated June 24th 1930 by the CME[7]. This contained two paragraphs explaining why "probably" *(sic)* the steam pocket had been created. The first was that the tubes across the roof of Fury's firebox were

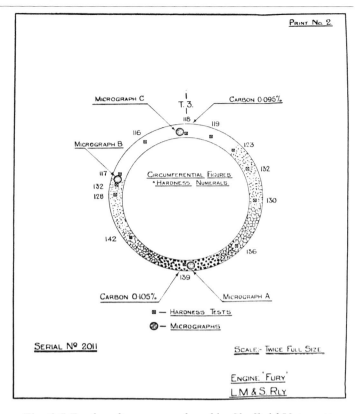

Fig..6:7 Further diagram produced by Sheffield University to show hardness values in transverse section of tube and points where microphotographs were taken of crystalline structures which were enclosed with the report. (National Railway Museum)

inclined to a much lesser degree than those in Henschel locomotive. The second explanation was that the brick arch support tubes had deprived adjacent tubes of water. Fowler's report then detailed the actions to be taken as a result of these explanations of the tube failure:-

> "(1) The tubes at the top of the box are receiving an inclination generally of 13 degrees, this being gradually reduced in the last 5 (bifurcated) tubes near the low pressure tube plate, where the tubes are not so exposed to the direct action of the flames.
>
> (2) The brick arch supporting pipes to be done away with, and a new type of brick arch to be provided. This latter to be shortened and given less inclination and to have rounded corners at the open end to prevent local eddying and high velocity of the flames......"

This report does not mention another modification which was carried out - not surprisingly after Carstairs – the fitting of self-closing fire box doors.

There can be no doubt whatsoever that these modifications represented a total rebuild of the ultra-high pressure circuit of the boiler. It was certainly no 'quick repair job' at NBL and hence supports the conviction that many of the images of Fury at Hyde Park with her boiler removed are from the post-Carstairs period and not during the original build.

We are left with several unanswered questions arising from both the Fatal Accident Inquiry and the Sheffield University investigation:-

♦ Before leaving Polmadie, Blair the fireman was unable to see clearly the level of the water in the ultra-high pressure circuit. He was told however that it was satisfactory. Who was negligent?

♦ Francis Pepper claimed to have seen a 'hair flaw' in the pipe that much later burst. Either it was a fantasy or something abnormal had caught the eye of an experienced engineer and draughtsman. He was not apparently challenged on this.

♦ The testimony of Thomas Lawson, the works manager at Hyde Park that the burst tube was 5.32 inches in diameter and the length of the split was 5½ inches long was patently untrue.

♦ Herbert Chambers believed that the thickness of the ultra-high pressure tubes "was quite sufficient to withstand the pressure". On what did he base his opinion? What data supported his belief?

♦ Professor Lea of Sheffield University appeared to change his conclusions. Did mild steel "creep" at 1800 psi or not? What did he mean by creep? Did creep manifest itself in the same way in both mild steel sheet and mild steel tube?

♦ Who was involved in the decisions to rebuild the ultra-high pressure circuit and alter both the tube inclination and brick arch? Did these changes result in the subsequent poor steaming of the boiler?

Possibly answers to these and other questions were generated but records of them have since been lost. One must wonder however whether the LMS were really interested in finding out. They had avoided culpability in the court and had paid the widow of Lewis Schofield some compensation although he was not even in their employ. Fowler's overall role and responsibility for approving the design and materials of the boiler as defined in the agreement with The Superheater Company was never examined.

All things considered, those involved in the Carstairs incident, with the exception of the footplate crew, escaped lightly.

Yet this was 1930 and the present day culture of corporate governance, hazard & operability studies and risk assessment did not exist. Fatalities at work were a common occurrence. What might be perceived in the 21st century as an inadequate response by the authorities to an employee's work-related death was just accepted practice then.

Once rebuilt, Fury underwent further pressure and running tests at NBL and it was presumably decided that the next phase of testing should begin in accordance with the agreement and its clause 8.

Whether the decision had been made to conduct these running tests at Derby before or after Carstairs is unknown. Fury had now been back at NBL for 17 months after Carstairs but on the 15th July she was towed to Derby and no doubt Glasgow was glad to see the back of her.

Meanwhile other events of significance had been taking place within the upper echelons of the LMS. In 1931, with Sir Henry Fowler in his 62nd year, the LMS chairman Sir Josiah Stamp, was anxious to replace him as CME. Stamp conspired to arrange lunch meetings at the Travellers Club between Harold Hartley and William Stanier of the GWR ostensibly to discuss water softening. The real purpose however was to poach Stanier from the GWR and appoint him CME of the LMS. On January 1st 1932 he brought in Stanier with a brief to introduce modern and more powerful locomotive designs, using his extensive knowledge gained at Swindon.

Fowler was noted for his interest in metallurgy and during his time as CME had persuaded the LMS to investigate the behaviour of copper in fireboxes. Ironically in the light of Carstairs, he had cultivated a reputation for being an expert on boiler materials and design. This was said to have provided the means whereby Stamp removed him from the post of CME by being moved sideways into the newly created and grand-sounding post of "Assistant to the Vice-President for Works (Research and Development)". The Vice-President was the co-conspirator in his demise, Harold Hartley.

Fowler was effectively to disappear from the scene although ironically in his new job he did authorise the purchase of a diesel shunter which became the first of many to replace steam locomotives doing the same task.

Many books and articles have been written about Sir Henry Fowler and there are equally as many opinions about his abilities as a railway engineer. A synopsis of the biographies offers this (truncated) appraisal [35].

> "One gets the impression that Fowler was an amiable man with a great interest in people, and although (like Collett) he appears to have

been less interested in locomotive design, (although more so than has been given credit) he was a considerable engineer with interests in metallurgy, a vital element in locomotive design, and in boilers, and it is tragic that Fury (the high-pressure locomotive) should have met with disaster due to metallurgical failure of one of its tubes. The paper on superheating must have been comparable with Gresley's one on high pressure boilers, and this emphasises that Fowler has been badly treated by commentators. His comments on George Stephenson are highly perceptive and contrast sharply with some of the rubbish written by intellectual minnows. Fowler was clearly a brilliant scientific engineer and he must have been extremely well-equipped to assess George Stephenson's extraordinary genius. He must certainly have been a most likeable man."

One is left to ponder whether Fury had been his nemesis

By the time Fury left Glasgow for Derby it was no longer Fowler but Stanier who would have control of her fate.

Footnote to Carstairs

Of the several other locomotives which were constructed on the Schmidt principle, the fate of the French engine is of particular relevance. This was a 4-8-2 express locomotive number 241.B.1 built for the P.L.M. Railway.

On April 25th 1933 whilst working a train from Larouche one of the tubes in the ultra-high pressure circuit burst. The burst occurred at about the same point in the firebox roof as that on Fury. The tube was of similar size and steel composition to that used by the Superheater Company and the spilt of almost identical characteristics. Analyses were carried out in much the same way as those by Sheffield University and with similar results. However the French investigators concluded that special alloy steels were essential for the tubes of such boilers and mild steel was wholly unsuitable. Additionally they added that even using chromium/molybdenum steel tubes would not prevent tube failure unless there was vigorous circulation of water within the circuit [31].

If there was a single conclusion to both Carstairs and the French failures it was that adequate water circulation in the ultra high pressure system was essential.

Fig. 7:1 *A rare (but over-exposed) picture of Fury at Derby taken shortly after her arrival. The old-type indicator shelter is being constructed and the pipe work from the cylinders for indicator diagrams is not yet fitted. (H.N. Twells collection)*

Chapter Seven

A MOVE TO DERBY FOR CONTROLLED TESTING AND FURY'S FINALE

Sequence of events, testimonies, and court enquiry, conclusions and LMS investigations

Contrary to the myth reproduced in many written accounts, after Carstairs Fury was not moved to the Derby Paint Shop and left there unused for many years. William Stanier, as the new CME of the LMS, was evidently prepared to see further testing carried out. We can only speculate as to his reasoning for approving this as he will have confronted many more pressing issues since his appointment towards the end of 1931. He was said to be no lover of compromise [44] and was not convinced that the Scots were up to the job of pulling the new heavier trains on the LMS routes. Only 18 months after taking office, Stanier had his first Pacific, 6200 "The Princess Royal" put into service, so he would have had little spare mental capacity for Fowler's Fury. Fowler of course had in 1926 submitted his own plans for an LMS Pacific with compound working. It was turned down unfortunately; had it not been, the story of Fury might have been very different.

Stanier would surely have been able to justify on many grounds that no further effort be devoted to Fury, it cannot remotely have been a priority for him. But whether subjected to pressure from others on the LMS Board or whether due to his innate engineering curiosity, he agreed to and supported what was to become 2 years of trials – in both senses of the word.

Fury arrived at Derby Works, most certainly not under her own steam, shortly after leaving NBL on the 15th of July 1931. Nothing is recorded of this journey.

As noted in the previous chapter, the entire high pressure system would have had to be rebuilt to accommodate the replacement tube, change in inclination of the tubes and the revised brick arch arrangement.

After some preliminary steam tests during which a new representative of the Superheater Company was always present, no doubt with more than a little trepidation, she began to be fitted with her testing apparatus. Outwardly, this consisted of tubes from the 3 cylinder heads so that indicator diagrams could be compiled and the ugly 'indicator shelter' fitted in front of the smokebox. It was behind this "shelter"

where the technical staffs were supposed to be afforded some protection from the on-rushing air. The job must surely have been one of the most uncomfortable on the entire railway payroll. For possibly several hours at a time, the men would be sandwiched between the crude wooden planking and the immense radiated heat from the smokebox door.

Documents from most of the test runs are preserved at the NRM, though these may not be complete.

The first brief published record of the testing is contained in a 1975 publication by W.G.F. Thorley wherein he reproduces the account of a LMS fitter at Wellingborough who was to become involved in the events [33].

Although out of sequence with events yet to be described, it is very worthy of scrutiny:-

> "This was followed by the incursion of Class 6 4-6-0 No 6399 Fury at the depot. [Wellingborough] After Fury had undergone modification following the bursting of a high pressure water tube, part of the 'wall' of the firebox, near Carstairs in early 1930, when the Superheater Co's representative was killed and the railway fireman seriously injured, it ran further trials involving use of the dynamometer car and production of indicator diagrams. The trials were conducted on Sundays from Derby on the main line to London. I do not know whether it was the intention to project them beyond Wellingborough, but the first one certainly terminated there when the feed pump which fed the high pressure drum failed in the vicinity. On the following day, Frank S. Pepper visited the depot to examine the offending pump; he was experimental draughtsman in the locomotive drawing office at Derby and seasoned in the wiles of the locomotive, as he had been on the footplate

Opposite page - Fig..7:2 Fury at Derby fitted with pipes from the cylinders for the indicator diagrams and the old type LMS shelter on the front. The rear-most inspection cover over the hp drum is missing, together with its fasteners. (H.N.Twells collection)

Above - Fig.7:3 Similar picture to above but Fury has been moved after running.

when the fatality occurred at Carstairs. I was scraping a regulator valve at a nearby bench when Pepper, an extremely agile man, jumped from the foot-framing at the side of the boiler to the floor. In so doing he caught the ring on the third finger of his right hand in a split pin securing one of the joint pins of the indicator gear, stripping the flesh down to the second joint. The coppersmith rendered first aid, but Pepper declined the assistance of the wheeled litter which was the pride of the shed and suitably accompanied made his way to the cottage hospital, where the finger was amputated under a local anaesthetic. By this time the engine was beginning to earn an unenviable reputation; quite apart from its poor performance, it was viewed with a wary eye by all who had to do with it. On its 'next trial, which was to terminate at Wellingborough, I was brought on specially to uncouple the engine from the tender should it

be found impossible to turn both together in No 1 shed's 55ft turntable. Total wheelbase of No 6399 was 52ft 9¼ in, but the difficulty was to balance the load on a table of an old design. I did, however, succeed in turning it in one piece. It was then recoupled to the dynamometer car ready for return to Derby, under the eye of Herbert Chambers, the Chief Locomotive Draughtsman at Derby. He chatted cordially about this highly unconventional locomotive, about which I had read so much. Suddenly there was a loud bang. Except the driver, we all moved away more quickly from the locomotive than, I suspect, we had moved away from anything for a long time. The first thought of the driver, a phlegmatic individual, was that another tube had burst; but nothing blew past the newly fitted balanced firedoor, which was contrived so as to close automatically if pressure built up in the firebox. By this time, seeing clouds

Above - (right) Fig.7:4 Fury, before or after another testing run at Derby. Early LMS indicator shelter still fitted, nameplate obliterated with grime, but is the man with collar & tie on the footplate possibly Stanier?

Bottom - Fig. 7:5 A later picture of Fury at Derby during her trials, she is now fitted with the newer, side entrance indicator shelter and has been given a bit of an overdue clean.

of steam issuing from between the engine and tender under the footplate, we realised that it was only the intermediate steam heating hosepipe which had burst!"

The second account of the testing was compiled by C.P. Atkins in 1978 who at the time was the librarian at the NRM [34] and this, together with archived material at the NRM, provides the basis of this chronology.

All trials were conducted on Sundays as far as known; the first taking place on Sunday July 10th 1932, which Atkins notes was "a roasting hot day".

At Derby, Fury was coupled to some empty passenger coaches providing a drawbar pull of 308 tons together with the dynamometer car giving a total train weight of 433 tons.

Two trips were made as far as Trent, returning via Trent North Curve, Sawley and Chaddesden junctions. There were four on the footplate; a driver and fireman from the Motive Power Department, a representative of the CME's department and Mr Boyes from the Superheater Company. The total track miles covered that day were just 37½ at an average speed of 29.2 miles per hour.

An impressive amount of detail was recorded in the interim report written on the following Tuesday. The summary findings though were not encouraging. Steaming was described as "not particularly good"; combustion as "not satisfactory" and the indicator cards showed that the adjustment of the valves was necessary. Coal consumption was "excessive" though the report's author acknowledged the route and continual stopping was not conducive to a favourable assessment and therefore no definite conclusions could be drawn on the all-important index of coal consumed per drawbar horse power hour. This was hardly surprising given the very short run, speed restrictions and several stops. With a total journey of only 37½ miles, Fury was being made to operate like a small suburban stopping train.

Some consolation would have been drawn by the Superheater Company's representative (Mr Boyes) examination of the firebox tubes - they were described as "quite satisfactory" [35]. But the writer added cryptically ". . . compared with the last particulars that were obtained some little time ago". None of the reports available at the NRM make any reference to such earlier findings assuming this was not a reference to Carstairs which anyway was hardly "some little time ago".

The next run does not appear to have taken place until Sunday, September 25th 1932, some 3½ months after the first. It would hardly have taken this long for Derby Works to implement the recommendation to "adjust the valves", so there was evidently no urgency about generating results.

The day's programme was the same as the first run – two runs to Trent, but pulling a slightly bigger load of 350 tons this time. The interim report filed the next day was also similar to the first [36].

Steaming was again poor, particularly in the low pressure boiler. Coal and water consumption was again described as "very high", qualified by the comment that on such a stop-start, short run this would be expected. One positive finding though was recorded – combustion had improved. However this was achieved by holding open the firebox doors "when required", against the new self-closing mechanism fitted after Carstairs.

Evidently modifications were now made to the blast pipe back at Derby, since the next documented run makes reference to this.

Atkins [34] stated that a further two runs to Trent were undertaken on January 3rd 1933 or 3 months later, but this author could find no record of these in the NRM Archives. As that day was a Tuesday, this may be an error.

On February 1st 1933, written permission was sought for further running from F.H. Frere, the Traffic Superintendent at Derby. This time a much longer run was planned for February 14th when 54 wagons plus dynamometer car would be taken by Fury to Wellingborough. The subsequent report states "the train worked was the 12.40 am Mineral train from Wellingborough to Derby". This was incorrect on two counts; it would have been 12:40 p.m. and the train would have been from Derby to Wellingborough.

The day produced a succession of problems, beginning with Fury's usual driver reporting in sick. In Atkins' reconstructed and detailed account of February 14th, he assembled information from several sources [34].

Steaming was reported to be "fairly satisfactory" as far as Trent but from there to Syston the pressures in the boilers fell progressively. Steaming deteriorated further as they approached Melton Mowbray. A planned stop enabled the fire to be rebuilt in anticipation of the heavy working ahead up to Oakham. A surprisingly large amount of clinker was removed from the fire suggestive of poor combustion of the coal from Kiveton Park Colliery in South Yorkshire that was supplied at Derby.

The situation became worse as they were nearing Oakham with the high pressure boiler down to 500 psi and the lower pressure boiler reduced to only 95 psi. The decision was therefore made to request Oakham for a pilot engine as the run to Corby would not be possible without assistance. Further delays ensued as a 4F 0-6-0 goods engine was brought up. As if this ignominy wasn't enough for the crew of Fury, shortly after a coupling broke back at the 7th wagon

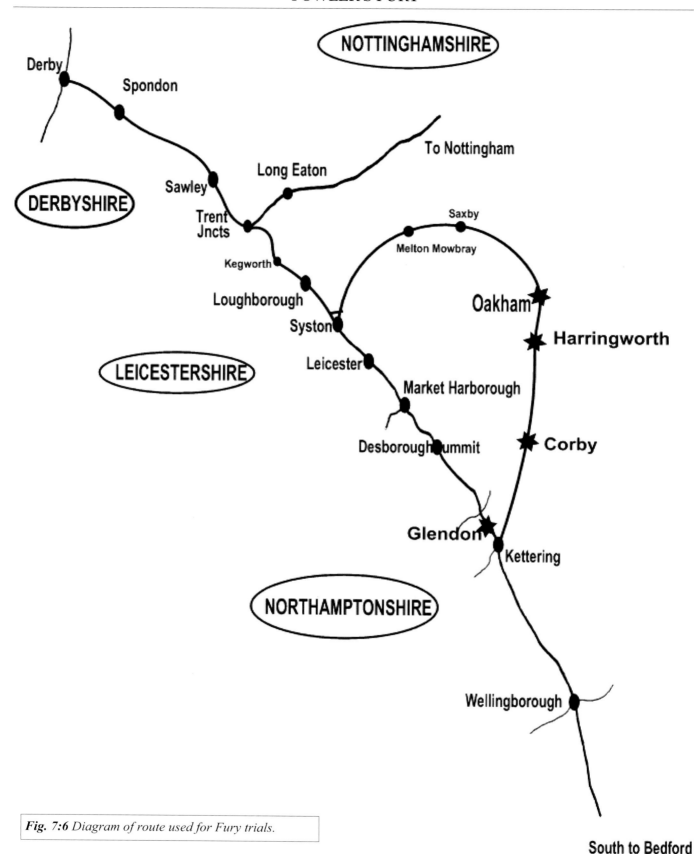

Fig. 7:6 *Diagram of route used for Fury trials.*

Fig. 7:7. Fury in the Derby Paint Shop again with the later type of indicator shelter fitted. (H.M.Twells collection)

from the rear. More time was lost as the 4F had to be detached to retrieve the lost wagons. The report gives Harrington for the location of this stop but it is another error, it should have been Harringworth, the site of the impressive Welland Viaduct.

Worse was to come; as they finally pulled away again the crew discovered that the left hand feed pump had failed and the right hand pump, although "working freely" was putting no water into the high pressure drum. *(These were the Knorr -Bremse pumps inset into Fury's smokebox)*. A stop was therefore made at Glendon, the fire dropped, and another locomotive summoned to take Fury and the dynamometer car into Wellingborough.

There was no realistic prospect of being able to repair the pumps at Wellingborough so the motion rods were removed from Fury yet again and arrangements made to "have the engine brought dead to Derby".

Needless-to-say, the report [37] of the day's fiasco was written up in a very negative manner. The writer noted that coal consumption was considerably greater than that of an ordinary *(sic)* engine working the same weight and speed. Despite the blast pipe modifications made prior to the run,

there was insufficient draft through the fire. His final sentence was a terse "It would appear that considerable modification is required in order to make the steaming satisfactory".

Four months were to elapse before the next run and by now four modifications had been made since her original move from NBL to Derby.

1. The blast pipe orifice had been reduced by 1/8th of an inch to $4^{3}/_{8}$ inches.

2. The chimney had been lined to reduce its diameter.

3. Holes in the brick arch had been closed.

4. The ash pan dampers had been modified.

So on June 18th 1933, a train was made up consisting of Fury, the dynamometer car and empty carriage stock giving a total weight of 363 tons. Another return trip to Wellingborough was scheduled along the old Midland Railway metals, a total distance that day of 127.4 miles.

Both driver and fireman had experience of Fury; the usual (unnamed) Derby Works observer and the Superheater Company representative rode with them in the cab. Fury had been steamed the day before and was still hot.

For once, Fury behaved herself, or very nearly so. The outward journey was accomplished in 90 minutes and the return, in 3 minutes less though there were booked stops at Leicester in both directions. The average speed was just over 43 mph. It was found that the steam pipe joint at the high pressure steam chest was blowing but nevertheless the report commented "Steaming showed a considerable improvement as compared with previous tests" and attributed this to the closing of holes in the brick arch. Much less smoke was produced throughout and combustion was said to be relatively good.

There was however a sting in the tail. The report [38] concluded that irrespective of the improvements, much still needed to be done before Fury was capable of hauling a full Royal Scot load.

Fig. 7:8 *Fury at Derby in early days: a head-on view over the pits (H.N.Twells collection)*

Atkins [34] records that on July 2nd 1933 (a Sunday) Fury took 318 tons to Wellingborough and back but provides no further information about this run. This is certainly confirmed by the next trial report (below) but no records of the event or Fury's performance were available at the NRM. The run had evidently prompted further work on Fury; this consisted of "the filling in of various air spaces round the base of the foundation ring, and at the top of the separator drums by plastic magnesia".

But it was not for a further 7 months that Fury went out again to find if these modifications had improved her steaming. Another trip from Derby to Wellingborough took place on June 18th 1933. Compared to the fairly successful run 13 months before, there were some encouraging consistencies. The fireman was the same, Grimethorpe Colliery coal was used again, the train weight was comparable (354 compared to 363 tons) and Fury had again been steamed the previous day.

It was not to be however. This time the report [39] recorded that although Fury departed Derby with full pressures in both high and low pressure boilers, after just 16 miles the pressures had fallen by nearly 50%. A signal stop at Syston enabled the crew to regenerate pressures but before long they were falling again. Even so they appear to have reached Wellingborough without further problem. On the return, the approach to Desborough summit found low pressures again and the speed dropped to 16 mph. Between Leicester and Derby the pressures fell even more.

Despite this, the report conceded that that coal/draw bar horse power/hour was consistent with the runs on July 2nd 1933 and the "good" run on June 18th. Water consumption by the same index was also identical to the earlier run. No mechanical problems were experienced and the fire was reported to be satisfactory and free from clinker.

The poor steaming must have been a frustration to the crew but one may wonder why the famous final sentence was written in such an emphatic style. It was to turn out to be Fury's death sentence:-

"As a result of the above tests the *general conclusions** which were arrived at following the test on July 2nd, can in *no way be modified**, the engine being definitely unfit for ordinary service."   (* this author's emphasis).

Regrettably of course, those 'general conclusions' from the July 2nd run cannot now be examined as they are missing from the NRM archives. It may be pedantry but it is worth observing that the sentence did not say what has often been reported [34,18], namely that "*the engine* could in no way be modified and that it was unfit for ordinary service".

Atkins [34] tells us from his contacts, such as The Midland

Fig. 7:9. *A further picture of Fury covered with grime at Derby probably after one of her steaming trials. The earlier LMS type of shelter is still fitted. There is now a linkage running from the vacuum pump to behind the indicator shelter which appears on other Derby photographs, Figs.7:5 & 7:7. (H.N. Twells Collection)*

Railway Trust, that two further runs were in fact made on March 25th 1934 (a Sunday) to Trent and back. However he provided no further details.

No photographs are believed to exist of Fury on any of her trials from Derby.

One incident was related by Atkins (*personal communication*) "The late Rev A C Cawston used to come in the old Reading Room at the NRM and he told me he was once standing on Trent Station in his dog collar when to his intense surprise 6399 steamed in, he was literally chased off the platform by an LMS employee. Even F G Carrier never got a shot of it either and he would have been in the know".

Fury was certainly returned to Derby and presumably Stanier at some point after March 25th 1934 decided enough was enough.

Though his source is not given, according to Sixsmith [7] Stanier wrote "*in spite of elaborate and prolonged trials, it has not proved successful, the steaming in every case having been unsatisfactory. In spite of continual modification there had been no signs of the boiler becoming an efficient and reliable steam producing unit or suitable for use on ordinary services; in addition, the coal consumption had always been higher than for any similar engine fitted with a standard type of boiler doing the same work*".

Fig. 7:10 *A forlorn Fury stripped of her indicator pipe work, valves and connecting rods but still with tender waits at Derby for removal to Crewe. (National Railway Museum)*

Whilst we might take issue with some of Stanier's conclusion – steaming was not unsatisfactory in every case – it was not an unreasonable assessment from a CME with better and more pressing issues to address.

We do not know whether Stanier had clear intensions about what to do with Fury at this point at the end of March 1934. His options would have included a new boiler and conversion to standard Scot but he was not enamoured with the Scots from the beginning and by now their running gear had become costly and troublesome. In that same month he had been compelled to ask for £46,000 to modify all 75 Scots then in traffic because of hot axle boxes and rough riding.

Nevertheless, just 4 months later it was being proposed that Fury be fitted with a new design of taper boiler and rebuilt as a Scot. This new taper boiler would then be fitted to all Scots "as and when their boilers fell due for renewal".

A whole year was now to elapse during which Fury was stored at Derby Works. With her fate now decided, at some point she would have to move to Crewe where the conversion would take place. Although theoretically capable of getting there under steam it was more sensible to tow given her track record. Accordingly the motion rods and valve gear were yet again removed together with all the pipe work for indicator diagrams and she was dragged outside when at some point, several photographs were taken.

In March of 1935 Fury was separated from her tender and coupled up to some undistinguished engine and towed, probably with other redundant stock, the 50-odd miles to Crewe Works.

At Crewe she was stripped and with little more than her chassis and wheels remaining, emerged a few months later as LMS no. 6170 British Legion.

Fig.7:11 Dr J E Simpson, a Cambridge academic, later presented these negatives he had taken to the NRM. He had thankfully thought it worthwhile to walk across the tracks at Derby on miserable March days in 1935 to record these final images of Fury. (National Railway Museum)

Fig. 7:12 *Possibly the last known picture of Fury, she waits amongst the scrap at Derby for her final journey to Crewe and renaissance (H.N.Twells collection)*

In the grand scheme of LMS finances, the cost of Fury to them was trivial. With the Superheater Company paying for the complex boiler; the construction cost was about £1,000 more than a conventional Scot. But whereas a Scot would be ready for service after handover, Fury was still incapable of earning revenue after 4 years on the inventory. As shown in Chapter 1, the mid 1930s still reflected the effects of the Great Depression. Earnings were depressed and so were prices. In fact, prices and earnings were lower in 1934 than they had been in 1924. Unemployment rose to about 22 per cent of the working population. The written-down value of Fury on the LMS balance sheet would have been insignificant.

Stanier had much on his plate; the costs of running the Fowler Scots had soared as coal consumption rose due to leaking valves and those other problems required him to seek money for remedial work. He was not getting on well with the very competent Herbert Chambers his Chief Draughtsman at Derby and was much occupied with the introduction of new engines. Consequently it is little wonder that he pulled the plug on Fury.

However Stanier had one last issue to manage with respect to Fury and that was the Superheater Company and their contribution to the whole affair. The Superheater Company, faced with a total write-off of their investment in the Schmidt boiler were pressing the LMS for some compensation for the £20,000 (equivalent to about £1.75 million in 2011) they had spent.

After some wrangling Stanier asked the LMS board to provide £3,000 in recompense. In fact this was twice the LMS maximum contribution set out in the 1928 contract.

The necessity to see events in a broader context means Stanier's other preoccupations in 1934 must be considered alongside his deliberations on the fate of Fury. To describe all the motive power challenges confronting Stanier when the decision to abandon Fury was taken is outside the scope of this narrative. However the internal politics within the LMS and new locomotive designs he introduced were very well documented by Bellwood and Jenkinson [42]. Stanier's focus on converting the Claughtons, the new Patriots and in 1934, the new Pacifics would have left him with little enthusiasm to address Fury's shortcomings.

Fig. 7:13 *Fury at Derby probably soon after arrival and refitting of motion rods following the tow. The brackets for the indicator shelter have been fitted as have all extra piping. The linkage from the crosshead pump has been fitted. This right-hand views shows various minor features particular to Fury which did not feature on normal Scots. These include the sliding cab roofs panels, whistle position and the absence of the two small cab windows above the boiler.*

Fig. 7:14 The reincarnation. LMS 6399 'Fury' becomes No. 6170 'British Legion'.

The drive for "superpower" from steam had undoubtedly declined. LMS finances were constrained but against this, the money invested in Fury would not have been great, probably no more than the cost of a new Scot. But even in 1932 the future for diesel and electric powered locomotives was becoming clear. William Stanier had come from the GWR where there was no case to be made for unconventional boilers when Swindon design had achieved so much without compounding. The Scots which initially provided such promise had already revealed weaknesses and anyway, Stanier was known to have a low opinion of the Scots' boiler.

By the third quarter of 1932, the Schmidt boilered locomotives elsewhere in the world had shown themselves to be troublesome to say the least. Only the Canadians were persevering with moderate success with their 2-10-4 engine "The Mighty 8000".

Ultra-high pressure had never been of interest to Swindon and Stanier had been steeped in GWR tradition for 30 years prior to his arrival at the LMS. Whatever his actual contribution, it was Fowler's Fury and Stanier had permitted 2 years of episodic work to demonstrate its competence. It is true that little coordinated expertise was devoted to Fury during her days at Derby and there were at least some signs that her performance was improving. But railway history is

full of abandoned projects where innovative locomotives were summarily scrapped and converted to traditional versions. There was no time for sentiment, if a locomotive did not perform or was unduly expensive to maintain, it was terminated. By any reasonable appraisal of Fury's performance, Stanier's decision to end Fowler's project and convert her to a conventional locomotive was entirely rational.

Yet we should contrast this with Stanier's own interest and commitment to the unconventional. After arriving at the LMS he developed one of the most unusual engines to appear in Britain, the so-called "Turbomotive" LMS 6202. By 1935, this steam turbine powered Pacific was put into traffic and to achieve this, Stanier would have had to devote appreciable LMS resources. It is debatable whether his initial faith in Turbomotive was based upon any sounder expectations of success than Fowler had when he conceived Fury. Nevertheless, by the time 6202 was earning revenue and showing promise, Stanier had already given up the idea of 'superpower' from 6399.

Fury of course never earned a penny in revenue for the LMS and as Tuffnel wryly observed *"Fury must have travelled more miles under tow than under its own steam"* [43].

When a special locomotive has been built, one that was out

of the ordinary and a bold experiment in attempting to achieve something new, a book will usually have been written about its story. Inevitably the author feels compelled to pose the rhetorical question "could it have been a success?" For Fury, Stanier obviously thought not and it is difficult to come to a contrary conclusion. The answer must surely be no, irrespective of the engineering skills that might have been expended had they been available. There was no theoretical flaw in the concept of steam superpower where higher pressures could produce higher efficiencies. The problem at that time was that the theoretical benefits could not be realised in practice because of inadequate knowledge about ferrous alloys and construction techniques leading to incessant problems. The results always failed to match expectations.

The Schmidt boiler concept with its ultra-high pressure and compound operation was tried in Germany, France, the USA, Canada and of course, Great Britain. In none of those 5 countries was it considered worthy of further development. Only in Canada was there partial success and they too came to the same blunt conclusion that any potential advantages were outweighed by unreliability and therefore operating costs.

The reality was that a well designed steam locomotive using a well designed firetube boiler and simple rather than compound operation in the early 1930s could match or out perform any of the new complex experimental engines irrespective of cost considerations. (A decade or so later, after proper testing facilities were available, modifications to the defective draughting of a 2-6-0 locomotive enabled its maximum power to be increased by 55% [45]).

Chapelon in France was the only engineer to conclusively demonstrate that compounding coupled with a relatively high boiler pressure of 300 psi and thorough attention to detail could produce better performance in a steam locomotive. But this would be not achieved until the 1940s.

But once the higher maintenance costs of complexity were factored in it was clearly 'no contest'. Therefore radical and ambitious projects such as the LNER's "Hush Hush", Bulleid's Leader, the LMS 'Turbomotive", the Reid-Ramsay-McLeod turbine and Fury have to be seen as examples of ambitious British engineering innovation which simply failed to live up to their designer's expectations. Sadly none of them was even to provide ideas which could be exploited by later steam locomotive engineers.

For a flawed locomotive with such a short and chequered history, Fury has generated a tremendous amount of interest over the years. Repetitive texts describing parts of her story and some of them perpetuating errors still continue to appear in histories of the LMS or of unusual steam locomotives. Models of Fury in various sizes have been constructed and still regularly appear for sale alongside frequently copied images of her in on-line auction sites. In the world of model engineering an indefectible scale model complete with Schmidt boiler would be unachievable and other attempts to symbolise Fury in steam so far bear scant homage to that original, magnificent beast.

APPENDIX: FURY ON TEST

The following text is a verbatim reproduction of the final testing report on Fury. The font used, characters and punctuation have been retained. The original document (a carbon copy) is retained at the NRM.

<u>DERBY SOUTH DISTRICT.</u>

<u>WORKING OF ROYAL SCOT ENGINE</u> - *"FURY"*

<u>WITH HIGH PRESSURE BOILER.</u>

LT.7/3/5

-2-

Dynamometer Car Test, Engine No. 6399 "Fury"
Derby Wellingborough, Sunday, January 21st, 1934.

Train Miles	127.2
Ton miles, excluding weight of engine	45029
" " including " " "	60389
Time running (Actual) minutes	192.1
" including stops (actual) minutes	212.9
Coal (excluding shed duties) :-	
Total weight lbs.	5180
lbs. per mile	40.7
lbs. per ton mile, excluding engine	.1150
" " " " including "	.0860
" " drawbar horse power hour	3.55
" " square foot of grate per hour	57.8
Grate area	28
Average running speed	39.8
Maximum " "	70.0
Work done by engine in H.P. minutes	875590
" " " " " " hours	1459.3
Horse power minutes per ton mile	1.94
(excluding engine)	
Water, total gallons	4650
Gallons per mile	37.3
lbs per ton mile (including engine)	.786
" " drawbar horse power hour	32.6
" " lb. of coal	9.18

90

GENERAL REMARKS.

On the outer run there were two signal stops, the actual average speed of the train being 39 miles an hour. The engine left Derby with full pressure in the high and low pressure boilers, and although the engine was lightly worked to run at a relatively low speed, the pressure had dropped

after running 16 miles to 680 in the high pressure boiler and 150 in the low pressure boiler, and the engine ran in this condition until stopped at Syston by signals when the pressure in both boilers was regained.

After leaving Leicester the pressure again fell and at Kibworth 165 in the low pressure boiler and 720 in the high.

On the return journey when running between Wellingborough and Desborough the pressure gradually fell away until approaching the summit (at Desborough) the low pressure boiler stood at 130 and the high at 600. Owing to these conditions the engine could not be operated in order to keep time, and at one point the speed had dropped to 16 m.p.h., 6 minutes being lost in running.

The actual mean speed between Wellingborough and Desborough was 29 m.p.h. against the relatively low booked speed for passenger working of 39 m.p.h. A further $2\frac{1}{2}$ minutes were lost in running to Leicester, the pressures before shutting off being 140 in the low and 720 in the high.

Between Leicester and Derby the pressure fell to 115 in the low and 610 in the high.

- 3 -

Dynamometer Car Test, Engine No. 6399 "Fury" Derby Wellingborough, Sunday, January 21st, 1934.

The average draw bar horse power exerted by the engine when running on the main rising gradients was as follows :-

A rare three-quarter view of Fury taken from height on 'official photographs' day at NBL. It was only used, as far as is known, by "The Railway Magazine" in February 1930 – it lacks contrast and sharpness.

Derby - Wellingboro'.

Section.	Average Draw-bar H.P.
Loughboro'-Sileby.	486
Syston-Leicester	606
Wigston-Kibworth North.	488
Market Harborough to Desborough North.	710

Wellingboro'-Derby.

Kettering-Desborough Nth.	411
East Lang-ton-Kibworth Nth.	573
The average for the whole of The test was	490

The repeated indications throughout the test were that any sustained work performed by the engine, even if at a low rate, would be accompanied by a steady fall in pressure in the boilers, and no improvement in the steaming of the engine had been effected by the closing of the air spaces previously described.

It will be noted that the coal per D.B.H.P. hour was a little less than on July 2nd, but was

practically identical with the consumption on June 18th, 1933.

It will be noticed also that the water per D.B.H.P hour was almost identical with that on July 2nd.

The engine was free from mechanical defect except that there was a slight blow at the high pressure piston gland. The fire was in all cases in a satisfactory condition, and was free from clinker on the bars.

As a result of the above tests the general conclusions which were arrived at following the test on July 2nd, can in no way be modified, the engine being definitely unfit for ordinary services.

REFERENCES / SOURCES OF INFORMATION

1.   Ross, D. The Steam Locomotive – A History, *Pub*. Tempus, Stroud.
        ISBN 0-7521-3916-2. 2006.

2.   Wolmar, C. Fire & Steam – How the Railways Transformed Britain. *Pub*. Atlantic Books, London.
        ISBN 978-1-84354-630-6. 2007.

3.   Cabinet Conclusion 2. Unemployment. 13 August 1920. National Archives

4.   SECOND INTERIM REPORT OF COMMITTEE ON NATIONAL EXPENDITURE, January 1922.
        National Archives

5.   RESEARCH PAPER 99/111 21 DECEMBER 1999 A Century of Change: Trends in UK statistics since 1900.
        House of Commons Library.

6.   http://classic-web.archive.org/web/20070115224612/http://www.therhondda.co.uk/facts/
        coal_prices_1840_1938.html

7.   Sixsmith, I. Royal Scots. 2nd edn. *Pub*. Irwell Press. ISBN 13-978-1871608-99-1. 2008.

8.   Bradley, R.P. Giants of Steam. *Pub*. Oxford Publishing Co. Yeovil.
        ISBN 0-86093-505-1. 1995.

9.   Reed, B. Loco Profile 8 Royal Scots. *Pub*. Profile Publications Ltd, Windsor. 1971.

10.   Court J.H. Model Engineer 141 3055. 82-87; 3506. 135-137. 1975.

11.   www.nationalarchives.gov.uk/currency/results.asp#mid.

12.   Boettcher, B. Second International Conference of the Railway History Association (IRA) / Association
        Internationale d'Histoire des Chemins de Fer   (AIHC). Lisbon (Portugal), November 27- 29, 2006.

13.   www.deutsches-museum.de/en/verkehrszentrum/information/history/transport-exhibitions/
        or
        www.travelbrochuregraphics.com/Advertising_Pages/Advertising_3/DeutscheVerher1.htm

14.   The New Zealand Railways Magazine. History of Superheated Steam — The Trend of Modern Development. 6. 7.
        1932.

15.   Proc. Soc Inst Mech Engineers. 101. 649. 1921.

16.   Dunbar, A.G. Stephenson Locomotive Soc. Journal. Jan. 1976.

17.   Proc. Soc Inst Mech Engineers. 109. 927. 1925

18.   Experiments with Steam. Fryer, C. *Pub*. Patrick Stephens.
        ISBN 1-85260-269-4. 1990.

19.   "Fury of the LMSR an Unique H-P Compound". Railway Digest International. 1. 4. 1971. (unattributed).

20.   Schwartzkopff-Loffler Locomotive Ultra-High Pressure Locomotive. Carbon copy report, Undated and unattributed.
        NRM Archives. Box LOCO/EXPT/1

21.   Holt, G. FURY the experimental high pressure locomotive of the LMS. Backtrack._LMS Special Issue No. 1,
        page 14._2003 (Issue bears no date).

22. LMS.6399/6170 - A Chronology, by Philip Atkins, Journal of the Stephenson Locomotive Society, September/ October 1989, 65. 739. pp 177-179.

23. Ultra-High-Pressure Locomotive for L.M.S.Railway. The Railway Magazine Vol LXIV p311. 1929 (January to June).

24. Experimental High Pressure Locomotive. The Railway Engineer. 59 – 60. Feb 1930.

25. Meccano Magazine. XVII. 7. 536. July 1932.

26. www.itnsource.com/shotlist//BHC_RTV/1930/01/01/BGT407150344/?s=Fury&st=0&pn=1

27. Double-Pressure Compound "Royal Scot" Locomotive, L.M.S.R. Railway Magazine. 66. February 1930.

28. TERMS OF AN AGREEMENT BETWEEN THE SUPERHEATER COMPANY LTD . . . . AND THE LONDON, MIDLAND & SCOTTISH RAILWAY COMPANY . . . FOR A HIGH PRESSURE TWO PRESSURE BOILER TO BE FITTED TO A "ROYAL SCOT" TYPE LOCOMOTIVE AND FOR TESTS, TRIALS, ETC. TO BE CARRIED OUT THERETO.
(NRM Archives, York (2011).

29. Engine Mishap – The Explosion on the "Fury". The Glasgow Herald, Saturday, March 22nd 1930. (source NRM Archives, York, 2011).

30. Numerous copy documents and photographs relating to the study of the burst tube in the ultra high pressure circuit by the University of Sheffield.
NRM Archives, York. 2011

31. Causes of Burst High-Pressure Locomotive Boiler. The Railway Gazette. 543-544. November 22nd 1940.

32. Documents and copy letters referring to the LMS agreement with the Superheater Company and NBL ca. 1931. NRM Archives, York. 2011.

33. Thorley, W.G.F. A Breath of Steam. Vol. 1. *Pub* Ian Allan London, (199pp.). 94. 1975.

34. "Fury" on Trial. Atkins, C.P. Railway Magazine. 124. 932. 579-581, 1978.

35. http://www.steamindex.com/people/fowler.htm

36. LMS document LT.4/10-5. Interim Report. Dynamometer car test – High Pressure Engine No. 6399 – "Fury". 12th July 1932. NRM Archives, York. 2011.

37. LMS document LT.4/13-4. Interim Report. Dynamometer car test – High Pressure Engine No. 6399 – "Fury". 26th Sep1932. NRM Archives, York. 2011
38. LMS document LT.4/11-6. Dynamometer Car Test High Pressure Engine No. 6399 – "Fury". 2 pages. Undated. NRM Archives, York. 2011.

39. Loco. Drawing Office, Derby. 26/3/33. No LMS document number. NRM Archives, York. 2011.

40. LMS document U,4950. LT.7. Drawing Office, Derby. Dynamometer Car Test High Pressure Engine No. 6399 – "Fury".5 pages. 23rd January 1934.
NRM Archives, York. 2011.

41. Court, J.H. Model Engineer. Letters to the Editor. p492. 16 May 1975.

42. Bellwood, J. & Jenkinson, D. Gresley and Stanier – A Centenary Tribute.
Pub H.M.S.O London. 1976. ISBN 0 11 290253 7.

43. Tufnell, R. Prototype Locomotives. *Pub* David & Charles, Newton Abbot:, 112pp., 1985.

44. Pacific Steam, Evans, M. *Pub* Model Aeronautical Press. Hemel Hemsptead. 1961

45. Oxford Companion to British Railway History. *Pub* Oxford University Press, 1997.
ISBN 0-19-211697-5.

46. Ross, D. The Illustrated History of British Steam Railways. *Pub* Parragon, Bath. 2009. ISBN 978-1-4075-7488-2.

Notes on primary sources of information

The Mitchell Library, Glasgow.

After the liquidation in 1962, the joint managing director of the NBL suggested that the photographic records be deposited in The Mitchell Library. This became the North British Locomotive Collection, consisting of about 9,000 glass negatives and around 6,500 photographic prints.

www.glasgowlife.org.uk/libraries/the-mitchell-library/special.../NBL.pdf

National Railway Museum, York

At its formation in 1975 the NRM inherited a wealth of material describing locomotive and rolling stock design, performance, testing and history. This came from a wide variety of sources, and is in many different formats, such as volumes, reports, files, record cards etc. The majority of these records were grouped together into what is known as 'The Technical Archive.' It contains, among other records:
Locomotive, tender and boiler record cards
Carriage and wagon records including BR wagon statistics, GWR stock books and various private owner registers
Correspondence files relating to various LNER locomotive classes and the BR (Western Region) gas turbine locomotive
Various specifications and order records
Locomotive testing reports and records.
Work on the Technical Archive is ongoing, as parts of it have not been fully assessed, and some material is waiting to be added.

www.nrm.org.uk/

The LMS Society

Society activities and interests are not restricted to the years 1923 - 1947. Their aims and objectives are stated as encompassing the London, Midland and Scottish Railway, its precedents and antecedents and most of their members have interests in and knowledge of at least one pre-Grouping constituent company and/or the London, Midland Region and Scottish Region of BR. The society states "we are proud of our record in the fields of research and publishing with over a thousand books and articles, having been written by our members."

www.lmssociety.org.uk/

LMS Records

The Oxford Companion to British Railway History contains a succinct account of the fate of LMS archives. It records that in 1926 an edict was issued to destroy "this junk" which had gathered dust at Euston. Though the order was not wholly executed, it is stated *(ibid)* that the LMS records at the Public Record Office, Kew is 'strangely meagre' and there, the largest of the "Big 4" companies is represented by the smallest number of records.

The National Archives of Scotland

The National Archives of Scotland (NAS) holds the largest written and pictorial archive of Scottish railway history. The bulk of the collection is made up of the records formerly held by the British Transport Records Historical Records Department in Edinburgh and passed to us by the terms of the Transport Act 1968 (section 144) (NAS ref. BR).

The company records contain minutes and reports, letter books, deeds and agreements, circulars, locomotive and rolling stock records, civil engineers records, station traffic books, accident reports, and staff records. The NAS also holds an important collection of specialised books and periodicals on transport subjects, mostly inherited from the old railway companies and dating back to the 1840s, as well as timetables, publicity material and a large series of engineering and architectural drawings.
http://www.nas.gov.uk/guides/railway.asp